Easy to Use

PICK UP & PLAY

# LEFT HAND GUITAR CHORDS

SEE IT HEAR IT

JAKE JACKSON

Flame Tree Music

mobile
online
in print

Flame Tree Music
BOOKS • eBOOKS • RESOURCES

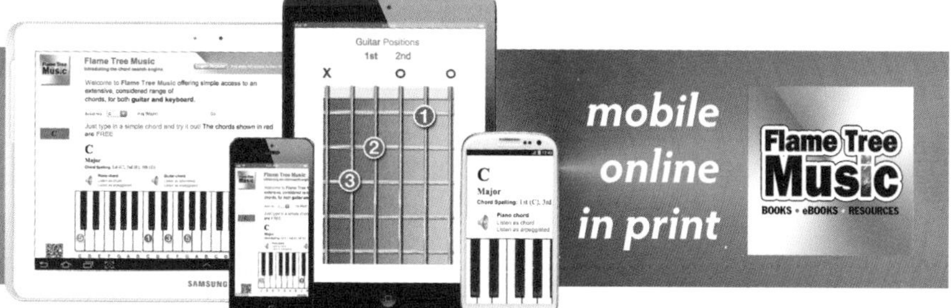

# Contents




**Publisher/Creative Director:** Nick Wells • **Project Editor:** Gillian Whitaker • **Layout Design:** Federica Ciaravella • **Website and Software:** David Neville with Stevens Dumpala and Steve Moulton

First published 2018 by **FLAME TREE PUBLISHING**
6 Melbray Mews, Fulham, London SW6 3NS, United Kingdom
**www.flametreepublishing.com**

Music information site: **www.flametreemusic.com**

18 19 20 21 22 23 24 • 1 2 3 4 5 6 7 8 9 10





The CIP record for this book is available from the British Library.

ISBN: 978-1-78755-236-4



**Jake Jackson** is a writer and musician. He has created and contributed to over 25 practical music books, including *Guitar Chords* and *How to Play Guitar*. His music is available on iTunes, Amazon and Spotify amongst others.





Printed in China

# Left Hand Guitar Chords

## An Introduction

**Chords are the building blocks for most music. Stringing together a few triads can liberate a melody and, being easy to communicate, will help you play with others. There aren't many books out there specifically for the left-handers among us, so we hope this one provides a valuable resource for left-handed guitarists.**

1. The chords are divided by key so that you can easily find the chord you want, work out what to play, and **hear the chord online**.

2. The chord selection focuses on those most commonly used – majors, minors, sevenths and power chords – but these are also joined by a few extras for experimentation: augmented triads, sus chords, sixths, and major ninths.

3. A chord 'spelling' accompanies each diagram. This is a great way to learn the structure of the sounds you are making and will help with melodies and solo work. Fingering guidelines are provided too, but these will often depend on what works for you and which other chords you're playing a chord with.

4. QR codes at the bottom of each page link to the relevant chord's page on **flametreemusic.com**. There, you can hear the chord strummed as well as each stringed note within the chord played separately.

5. All chords are shown in the first position, but you can see them in the second position too on **flametreemusic.com**.

This book aims to keep things simple so you can get started straight away with all the most useful chords. Whether it's for trying out new chord progressions, playing in a group, or writing your own songs, this chord book is designed to help left-handed players get the most out of their guitar!

# The Diagrams
## A Quick Guide

**The chord diagrams are designed for quick access and ease of use. You can flick through the book using the tabs on the side to find the right key, then use the finger positions and fretboard to help you make the chord.**

Each chord is provided with a *Chord Spelling* to help you check each note. This is a great way to learn the structure of the sounds you are making and will help with melodies and solo work.

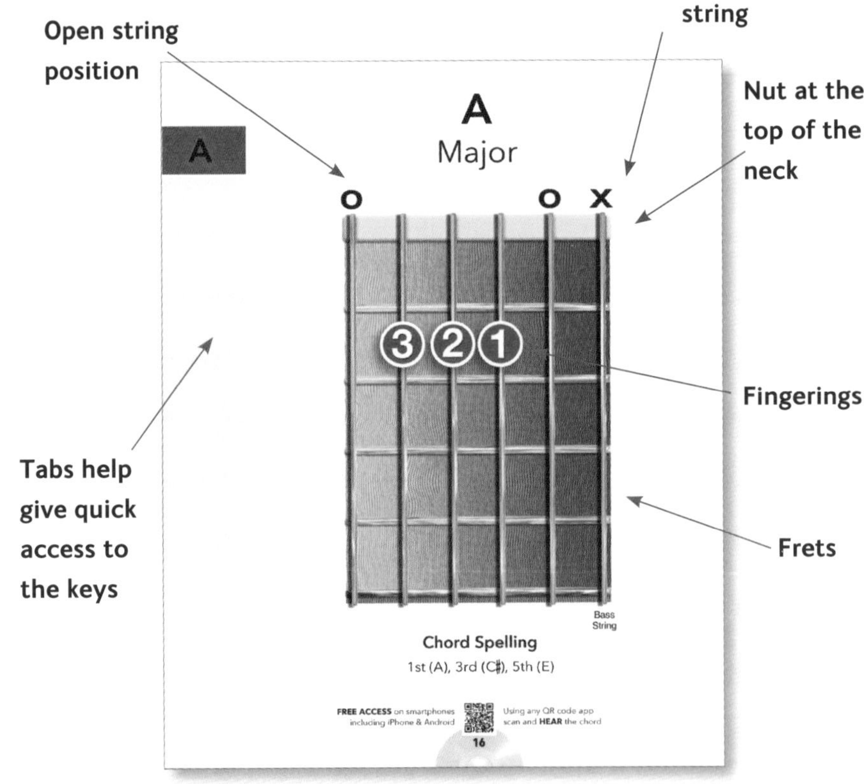


**FREE ACCESS** on smartphones including iPhone & Android

Using any free QR code app, scan and **HEAR** the chord

# The Basics

**Chord Name**: Each chord is given a short and complete name, for example the short name C°7 is properly known as C Diminished 7th.

**The Strings**: The **bass E** appears on the right, the top E is on the left (the top E is the E above **middle C** on the piano).

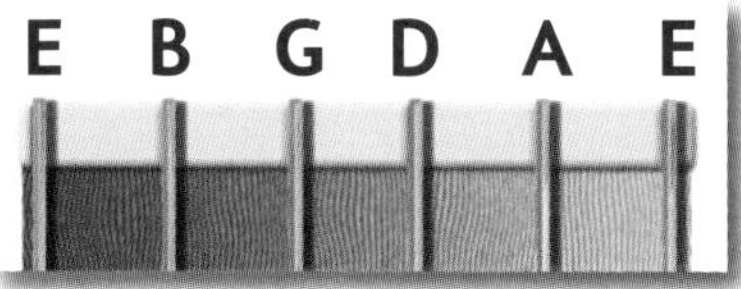


**Fingerings**: ❶ is the index finger ❷ is the middle finger ❸ is the ring finger ❹ is the little finger

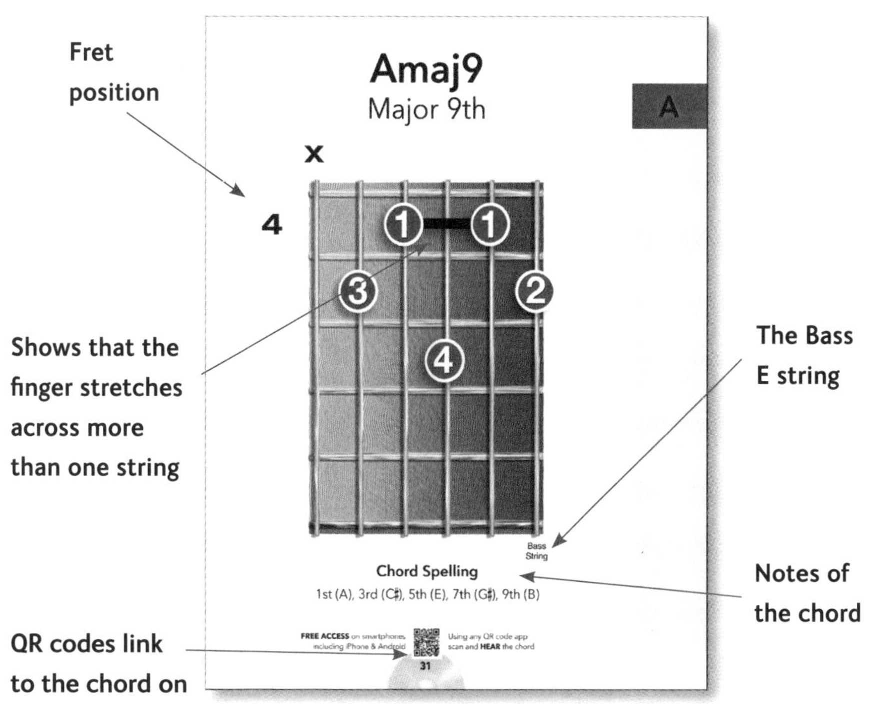


**FREE ACCESS** on smartphones including iPhone & Android

Using any free QR code app, scan and **HEAR** the chord

# The Sound Links
## Another Quick Guide

**Requirements**: a camera and internet-ready smartphone (e.g. **iPhone**, any **Android** phone (e.g. **Samsung Galaxy**), **Nokia Lumia**, or **camera-enabled tablet** such as the **iPad Mini**). The best result is achieved using a WIFI connection.

1. Download any **free QR code reader**. An app store search will reveal a great many of these, so obviously it's best to go with the ones with the highest ratings and don't be afraid to try a few before you settle on the one that works best for you. Tapmedia's QR Reader app is good, or ATT Scanner (used below) or QR Media. Some of the free apps have ads, which can be annoying.

2. On your smartphone, open the app and **scan** the **QR code** at the base of any particular page.

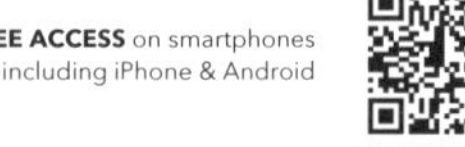

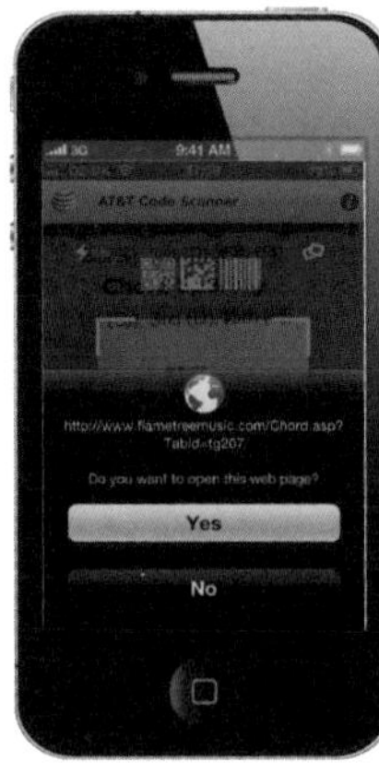


3. The QR reader app will take you to a browser, then the specific chord will be displayed on flametreemusic.com.

4. Use the drop-down menu to choose from **20 scales** or 12 **free chords** (50 with subscription) per key.

**FREE ACCESS** on smartphones including iPhone & Android

Using any free QR code app, scan and **HEAR** the chord

5. Access the left-hand guitar diagrams by selecting the '1stLH' or '2ndLH' options under 'Guitar Positions'.

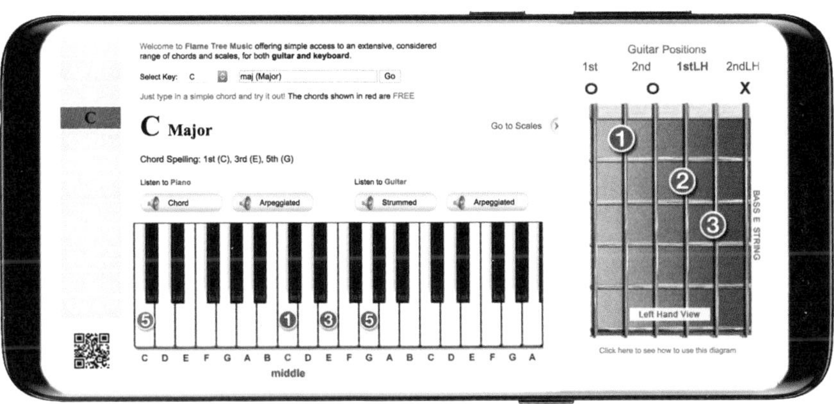


6. Click the sounds! Both piano and guitar audio is provided. This is particularly helpful when you're playing with others.

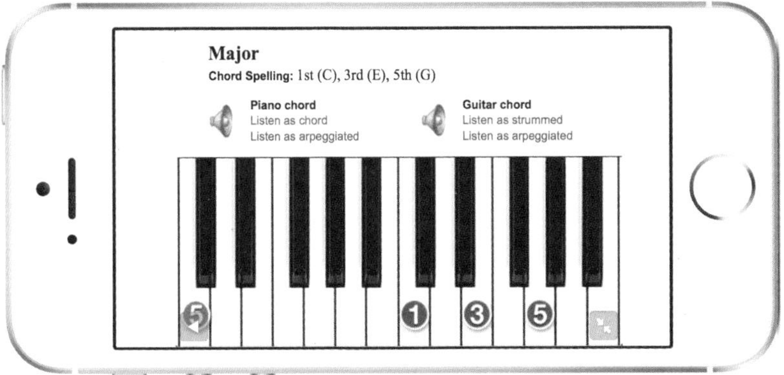


**The QR codes give you direct access to chords and scales. You can access a much wider range of chords if you register and subscribe.**

**FREE ACCESS** on smartphones including iPhone & Android

Using any free QR code app, scan and **HEAR** the chord

# A
## Major

**Chord Spelling**

1st (A), 3rd (C♯), 5th (E)

**FREE ACCESS** on smartphones including iPhone & Android

Using any free QR code app, scan and **HEAR** the chord

# Am
## Minor

Bass String

**Chord Spelling**

1st (A), ♭3rd (C), 5th (E)

**FREE ACCESS** on smartphones including iPhone & Android

Using any free QR code app, scan and **HEAR** the chord

# A+

## Augmented Triad

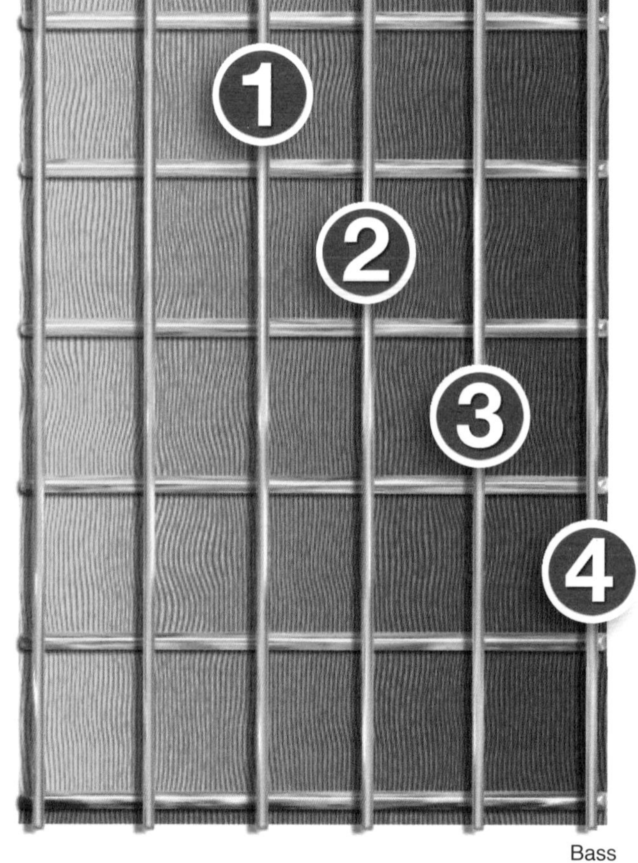


**Chord Spelling**

1st (A), 3rd (C♯), ♯5th (E♯)

**FREE ACCESS** on smartphones including iPhone & Android

Using any free QR code app, scan and **HEAR** the chord

# A°

## Diminished Triad

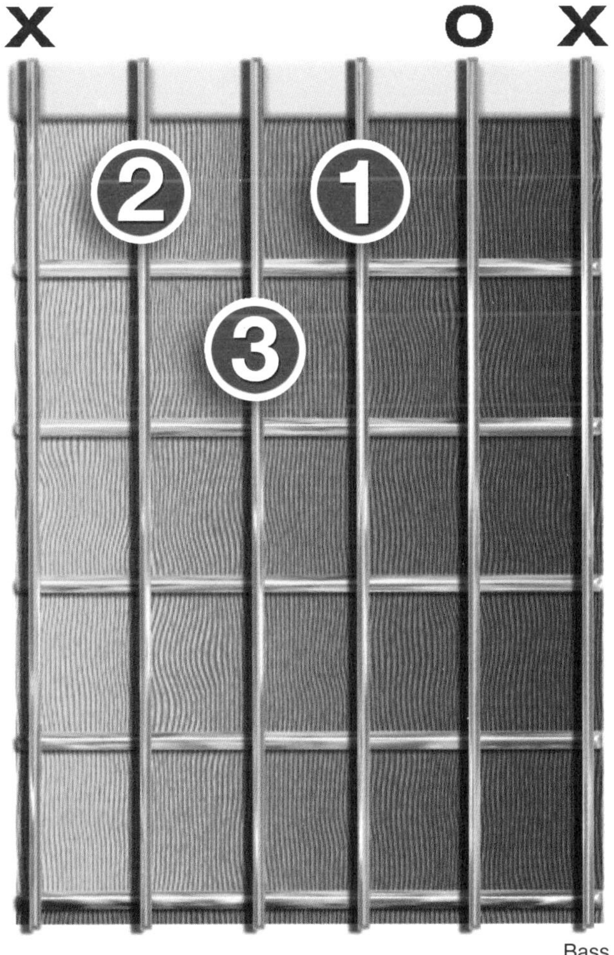


### Chord Spelling

1st (A), ♭3rd (C), ♭5th (E♭)

**FREE ACCESS** on smartphones including iPhone & Android

Using any free QR code app, scan and **HEAR** the chord

# Asus2

## Suspended 2nd

**Chord Spelling**

1st (A), 2nd (B), 5th (E)

**FREE ACCESS** on smartphones including iPhone & Android

Using any free QR code app, scan and **HEAR** the chord

# Asus4

## Suspended 4th

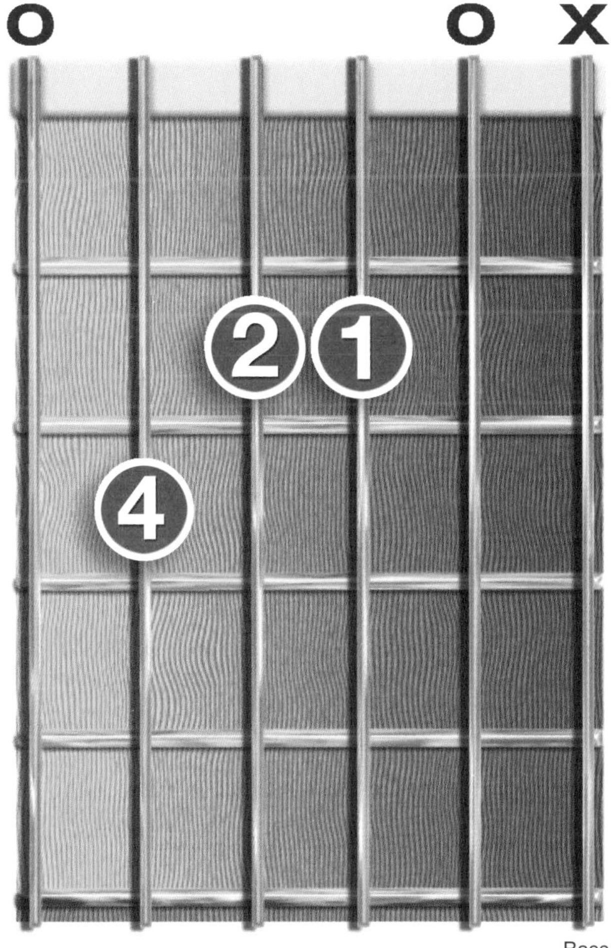


### Chord Spelling

1st (A), 4th (D), 5th (E)

**FREE ACCESS** on smartphones including iPhone & Android

Using any free QR code app, scan and **HEAR** the chord

# A5

## 5th (Power Chord)

### Chord Spelling

1st (A), 5th (E)

**FREE ACCESS** on smartphones including iPhone & Android

Using any free QR code app, scan and **HEAR** the chord

# A6
## Major 6th

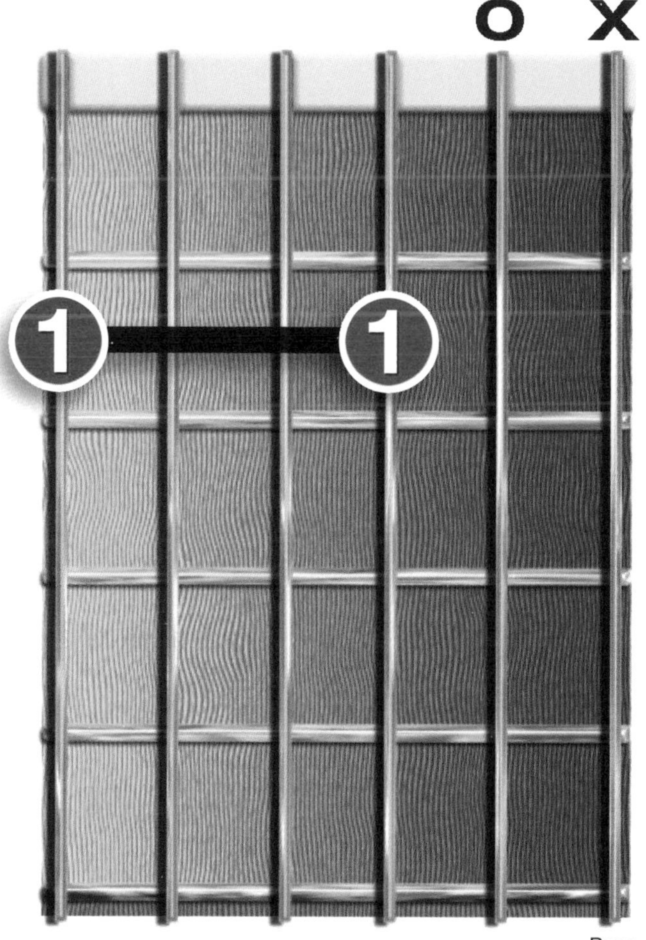


**Chord Spelling**

1st (A), 3rd (C♯), 5th (E), 6th (F♯)

**FREE ACCESS** on smartphones including iPhone & Android

Using any free QR code app, scan and **HEAR** the chord

# Am6

## Minor 6th

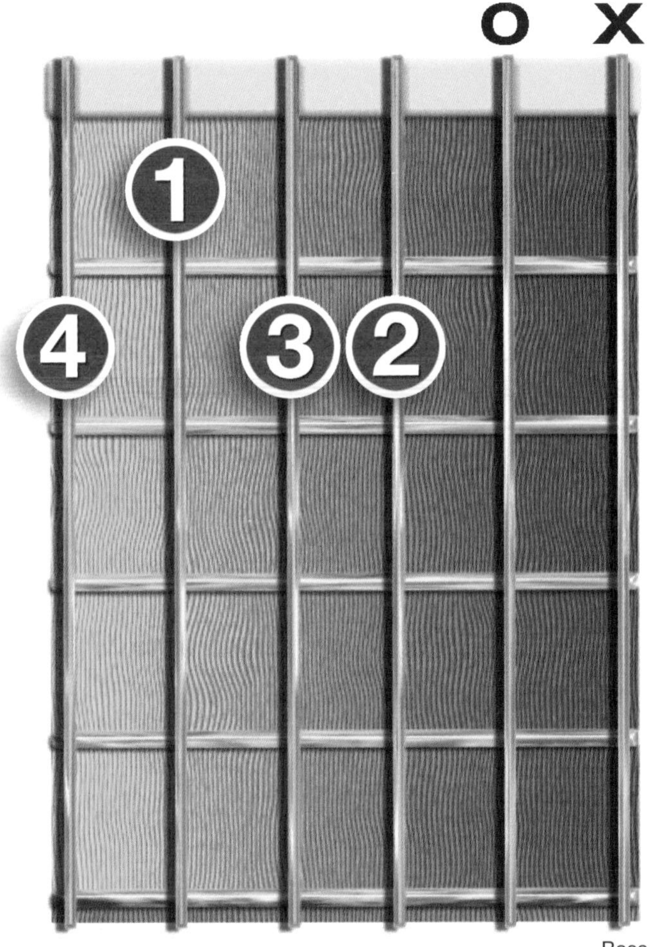


**Chord Spelling**

1st (A), ♭3rd (C), 5th (E), 6th (F♯)

**FREE ACCESS** on smartphones including iPhone & Android

Using any free QR code app, scan and **HEAR** the chord

# Amaj7

## Major 7th

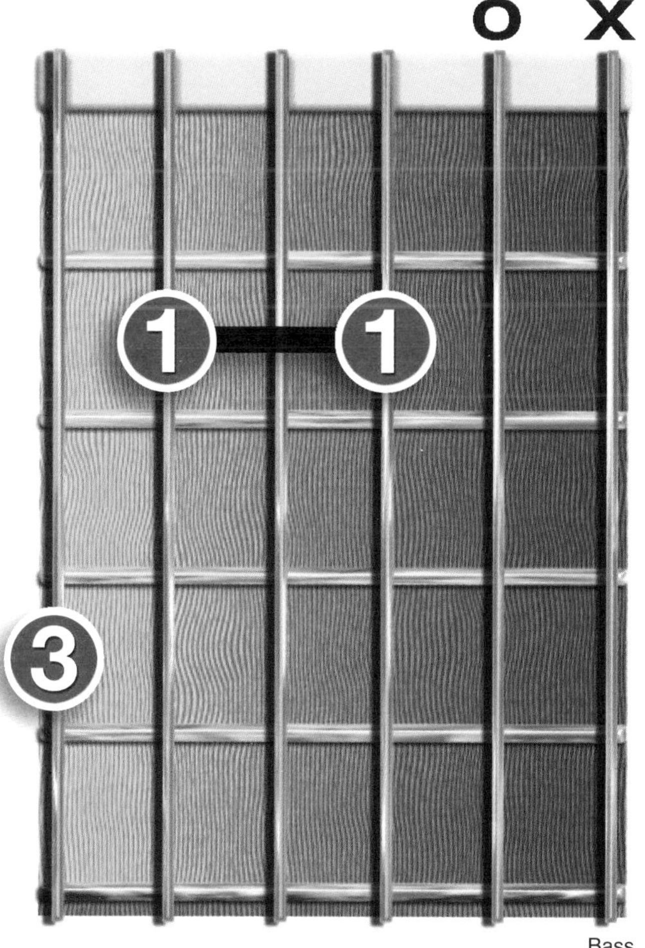


**Chord Spelling**

1st (A), 3rd (C♯), 5th (E), 7th (G♯)

**FREE ACCESS** on smartphones including iPhone & Android

Using any free QR code app, scan and **HEAR** the chord

# Am7

## Minor 7th

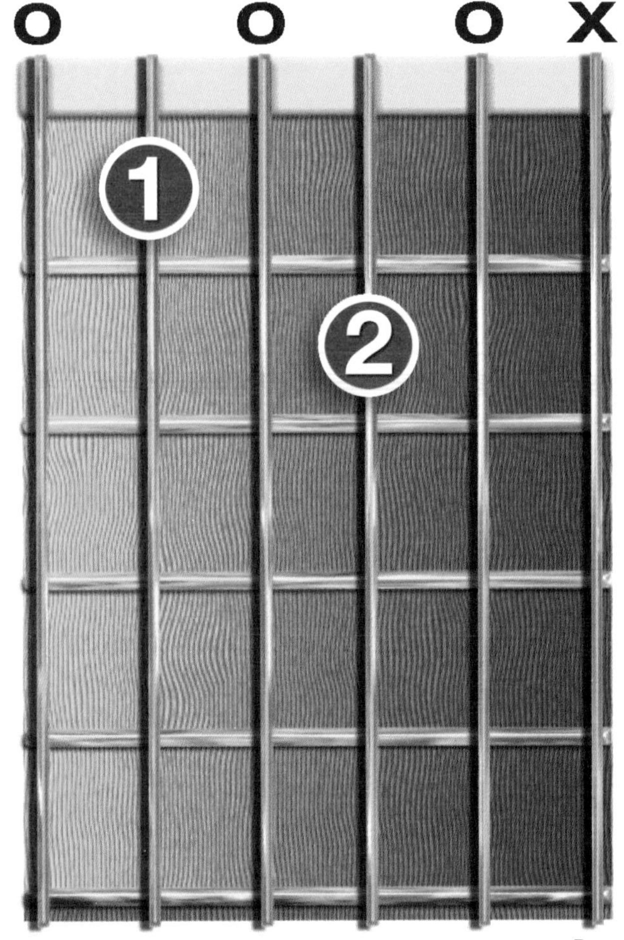


**Chord Spelling**

1st (A), ♭3rd (C), 5th (E), ♭7th (G)

**FREE ACCESS** on smartphones including iPhone & Android

Using any free QR code app, scan and **HEAR** the chord

# A7

## Dominant 7th

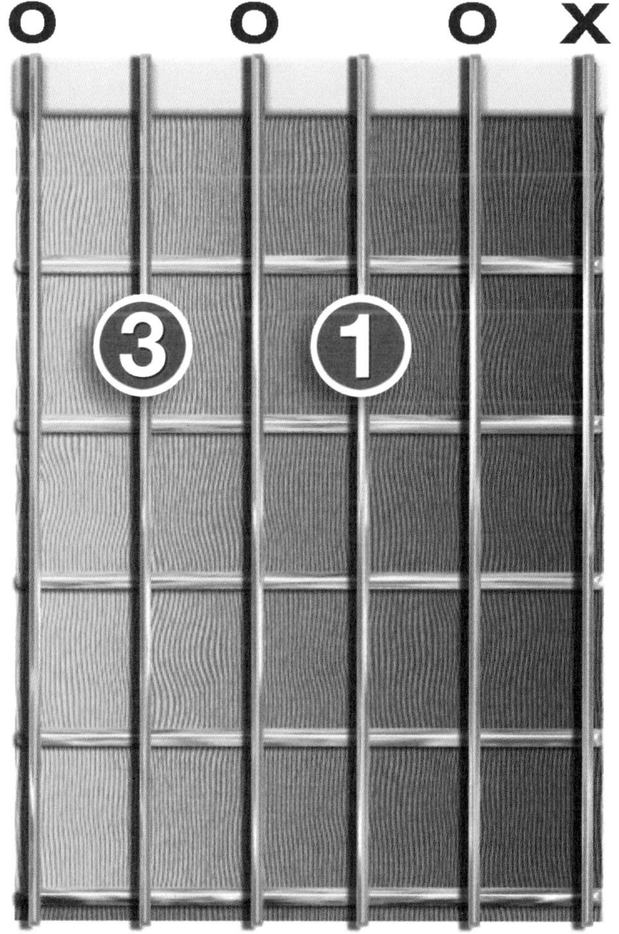


**Chord Spelling**

1st (A), 3rd (C♯), 5th (E), ♭7th (G)

**FREE ACCESS** on smartphones including iPhone & Android

Using any free QR code app, scan and **HEAR** the chord

A
A♯/B♭
B
C
C♯/D♭
D
D♯/E♭
E
F
F♯/G♭
G
G♯/A♭

# A°7

## Diminished 7th

x x

4

Bass String

**Chord Spelling**

1st (A), ♭3rd (C), ♭5th (E♭), 𝄫7th (G♭)

**FREE ACCESS** on smartphones including iPhone & Android

Using any free QR code app, scan and **HEAR** the chord

# Amaj9

## Major 9th

x

4

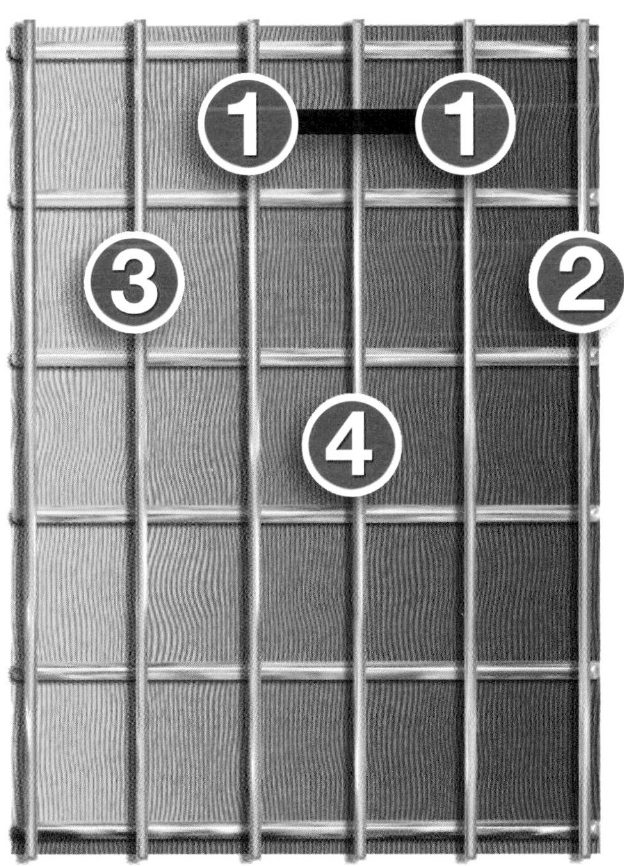


Bass String

**Chord Spelling**

1st (A), 3rd (C♯), 5th (E), 7th (G♯), 9th (B)

**FREE ACCESS** on smartphones including iPhone & Android

Using any free QR code app, scan and **HEAR** the chord

# A♯/B♭
## Major

**Chord Spelling**

1st (B♭), 3rd (D), 5th (F)

**FREE ACCESS** on smartphones including iPhone & Android

Using any free QR code app, scan and **HEAR** the chord

# A♯/B♭m
## Minor

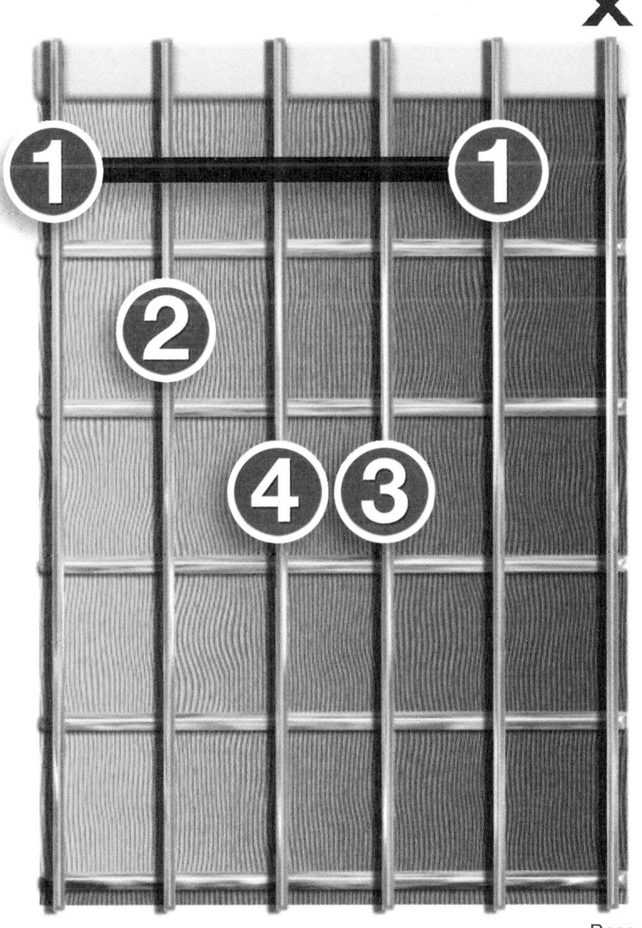


**Chord Spelling**

1st (B♭), ♭3rd (D♭), 5th (F)

**FREE ACCESS** on smartphones including iPhone & Android

Using any free QR code app, scan and **HEAR** the chord

# A♯/B♭+

## Augmented Triad

x x

3

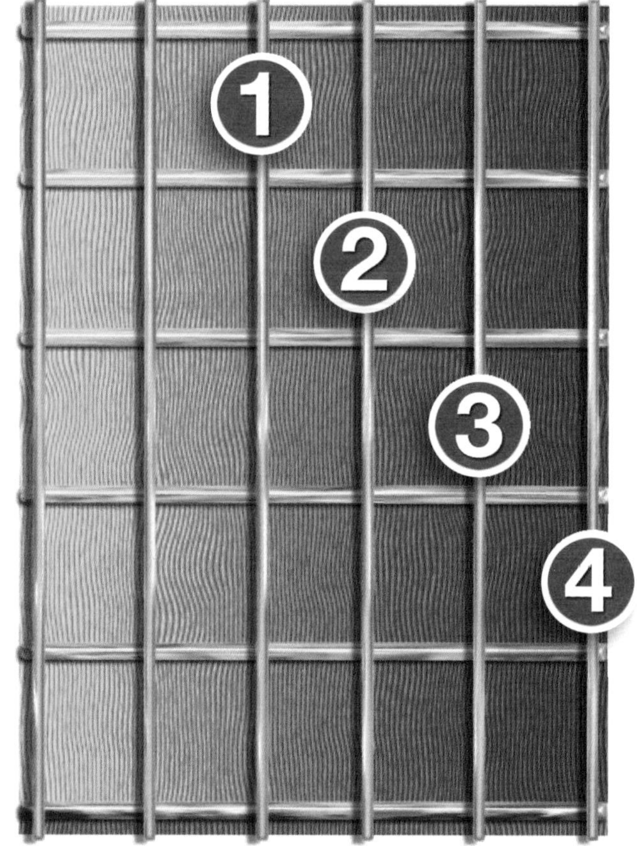


**Chord Spelling**

1st (B♭), 3rd (D), ♯5th (F♯)

**FREE ACCESS** on smartphones including iPhone & Android

Using any free QR code app, scan and **HEAR** the chord

# A♯/B♭°
## Diminished Triad

**Chord Spelling**

1st (B♭), ♭3rd (D♭), ♭5th (F♭)

**FREE ACCESS** on smartphones including iPhone & Android

Using any free QR code app, scan and **HEAR** the chord

# A♯/B♭sus2
## Suspended 2nd

Bass String

**Chord Spelling**

1st (B♭), 2nd (C), 5th (F)

**FREE ACCESS** on smartphones including iPhone & Android

Using any free QR code app, scan and **HEAR** the chord

# A♯/B♭sus4

## Suspended 4th

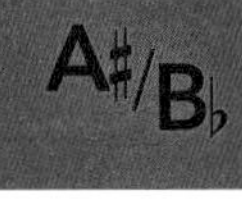


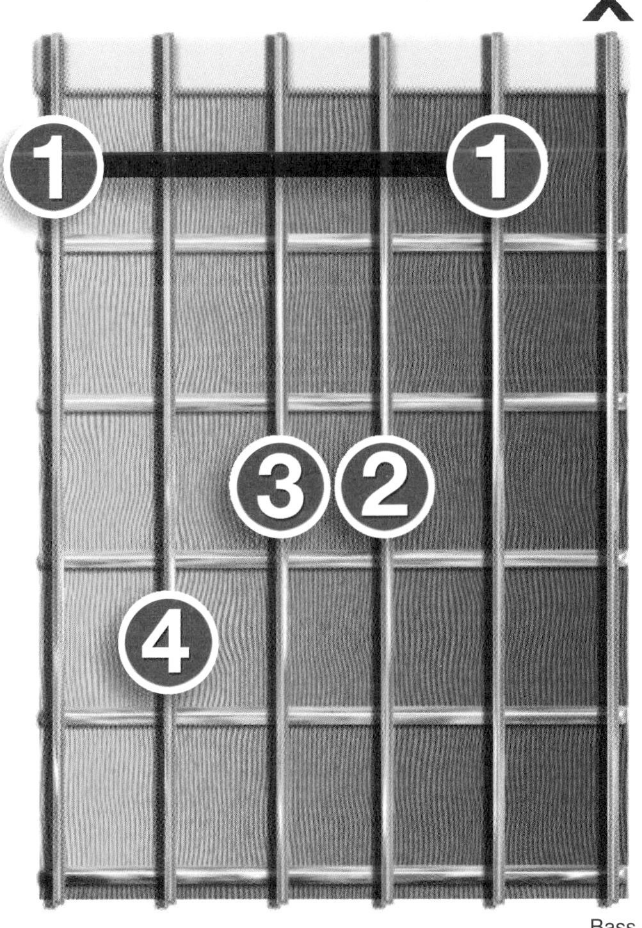


### Chord Spelling

1st (B♭), 4th (E♭), 5th (F)

**FREE ACCESS** on smartphones including iPhone & Android

Using any free QR code app, scan and **HEAR** the chord

# A♯/B♭5

## 5th (Power Chord)

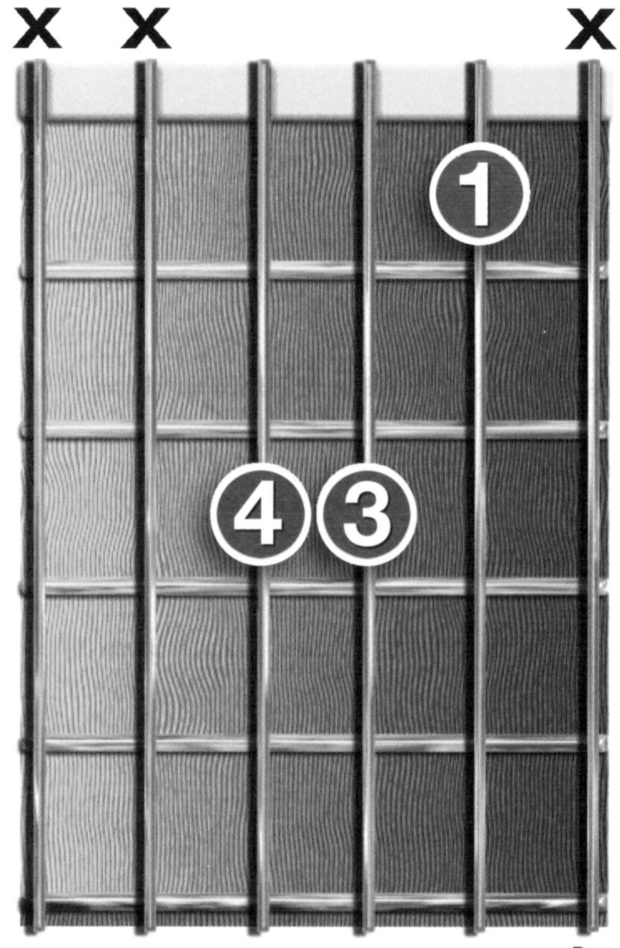


### Chord Spelling

1st (B♭), 5th (F)

**FREE ACCESS** on smartphones including iPhone & Android

Using any free QR code app, scan and **HEAR** the chord

# A♯/B♭6

## Major 6th

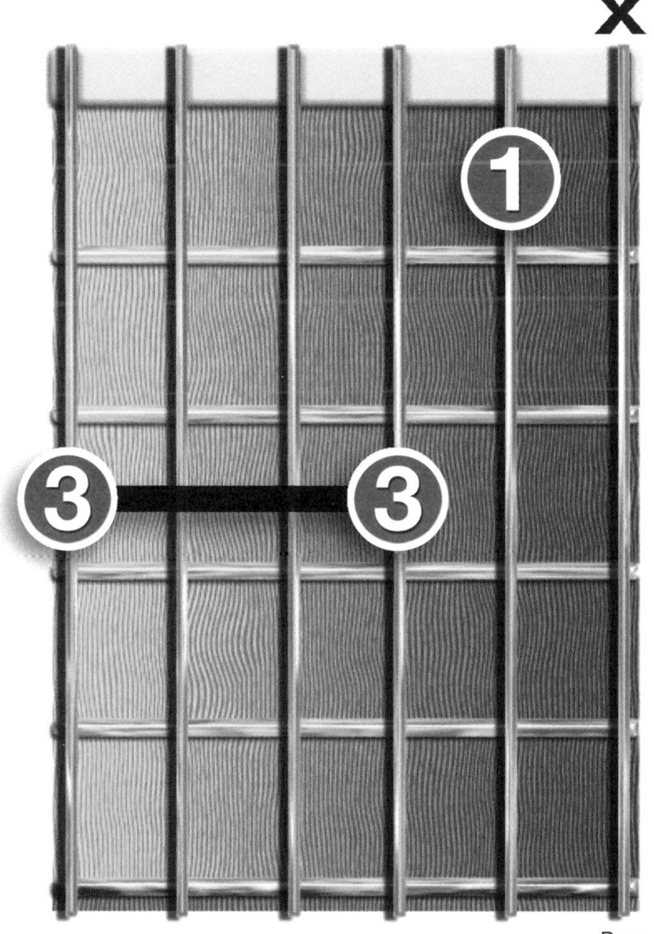


### Chord Spelling

1st (B♭), 3rd (D), 5th (F), 6th (G)

**FREE ACCESS** on smartphones including iPhone & Android

Using any free QR code app, scan and **HEAR** the chord

# A♯/B♭m6

## Minor 6th

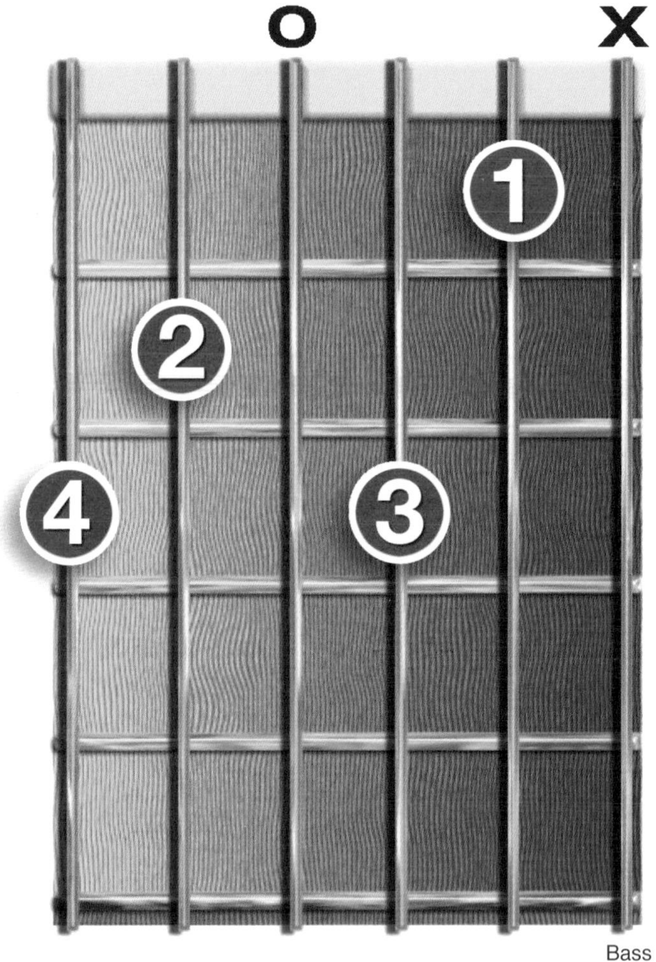


**Chord Spelling**

1st (B♭), ♭3rd (D♭), 5th (F), 6th (G)

**FREE ACCESS** on smartphones including iPhone & Android

Using any free QR code app, scan and **HEAR** the chord

# A♯/B♭maj7

## Major 7th



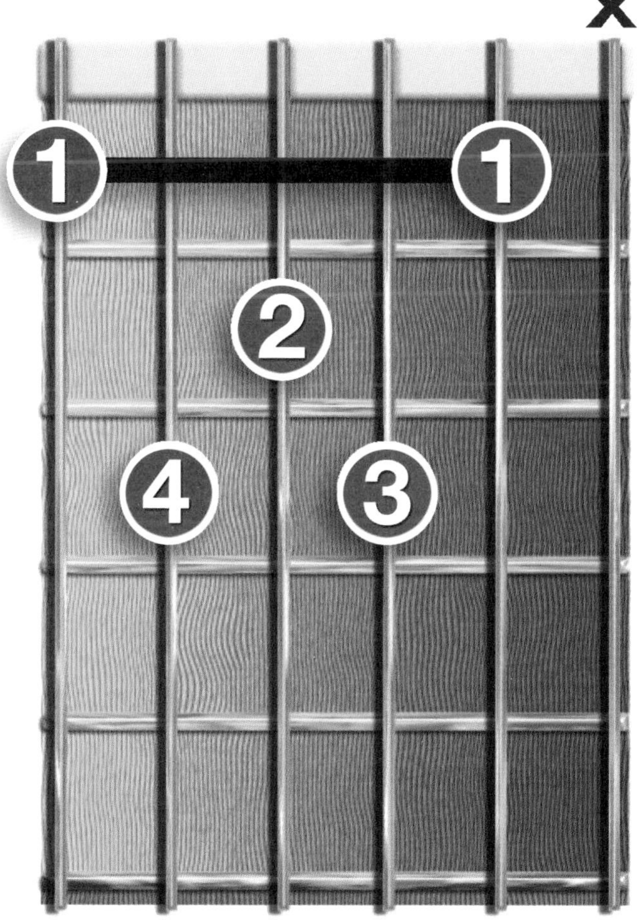


### Chord Spelling

1st (B♭), 3rd (D), 5th (F), 7th (A)

**FREE ACCESS** on smartphones including iPhone & Android

Using any free QR code app, scan and **HEAR** the chord

# A♯/B♭m7
## Minor 7th

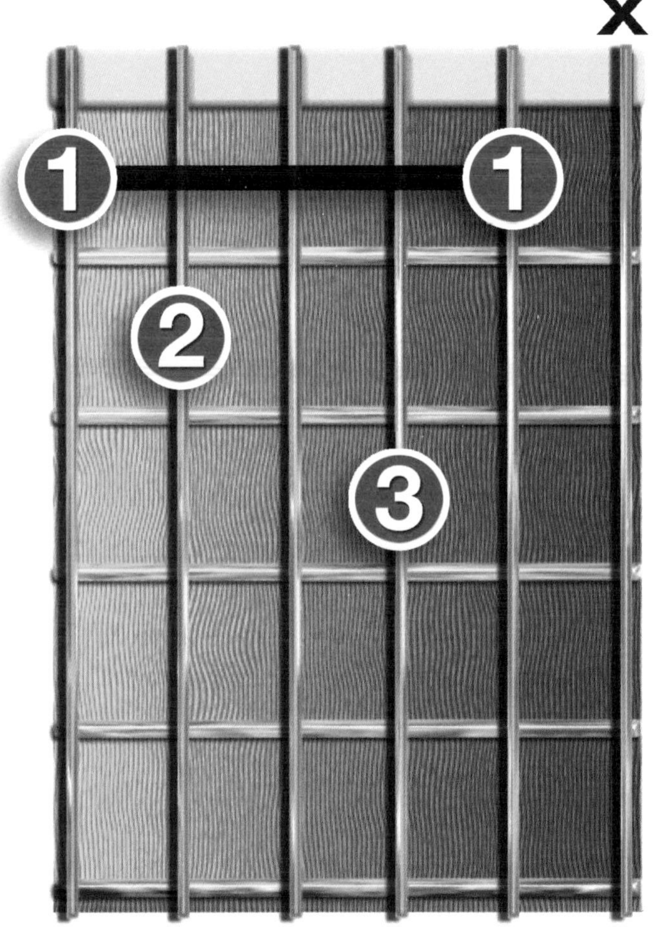


**Chord Spelling**

1st (B♭), ♭3rd (D♭), 5th (F), ♭7th (A♭)

**FREE ACCESS** on smartphones including iPhone & Android

Using any free QR code app, scan and **HEAR** the chord

# A♯/B♭7
## Dominant 7th

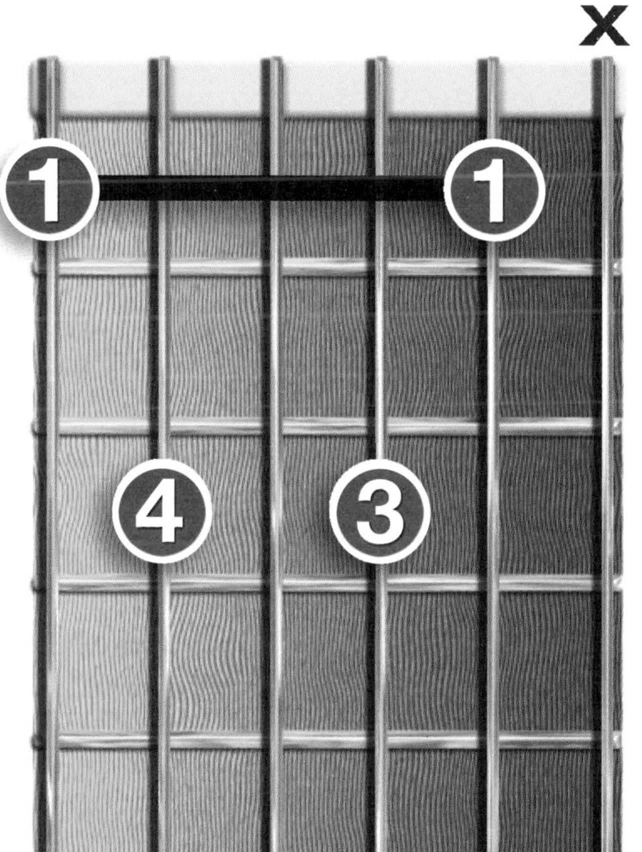


**Chord Spelling**

1st (B♭), 3rd (D), 5th (F), ♭7th (A♭)

**FREE ACCESS** on smartphones including iPhone & Android

Using any free QR code app, scan and **HEAR** the chord

# A♯/B♭°7

## Diminished 7th

**Chord Spelling**

1st (B♭), ♭3rd (D♭), ♭5th (F♭), 𝄫7th (A𝄫)

**FREE ACCESS** on smartphones including iPhone & Android

Using any free QR code app, scan and **HEAR** the chord

# A♯/B♭maj9

## Major 9th

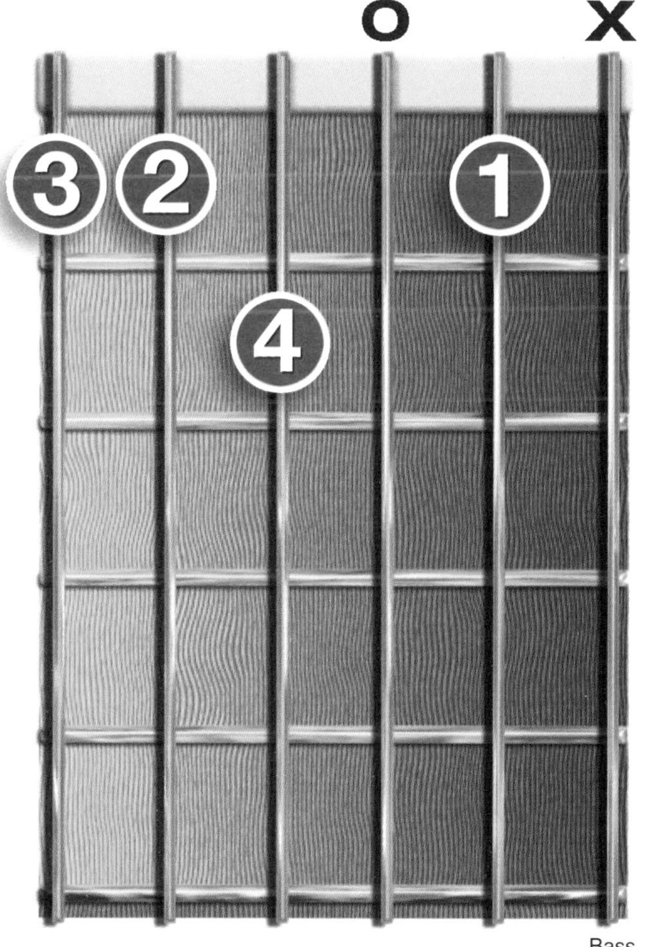


### Chord Spelling

1st (B♭), 3rd (D), 5th (F), 7th (A), 9th (C)

**FREE ACCESS** on smartphones including iPhone & Android

Using any free QR code app, scan and **HEAR** the chord

A
A♯/B♭
B
C
C♯/D♭
D
D♯/E♭
E
F
F♯/G♭
G
G♯/A♭

# B

## Major

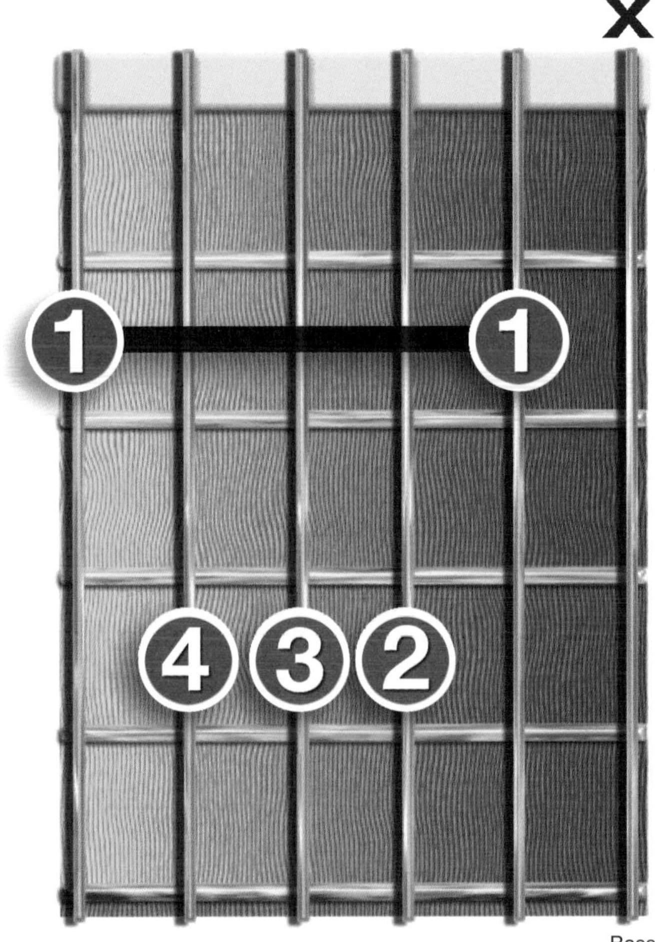


**Chord Spelling**

1st (B), 3rd (D♯), 5th (F♯)

**FREE ACCESS** on smartphones including iPhone & Android

Using any free QR code app, scan and **HEAR** the chord

# Bm
## Minor

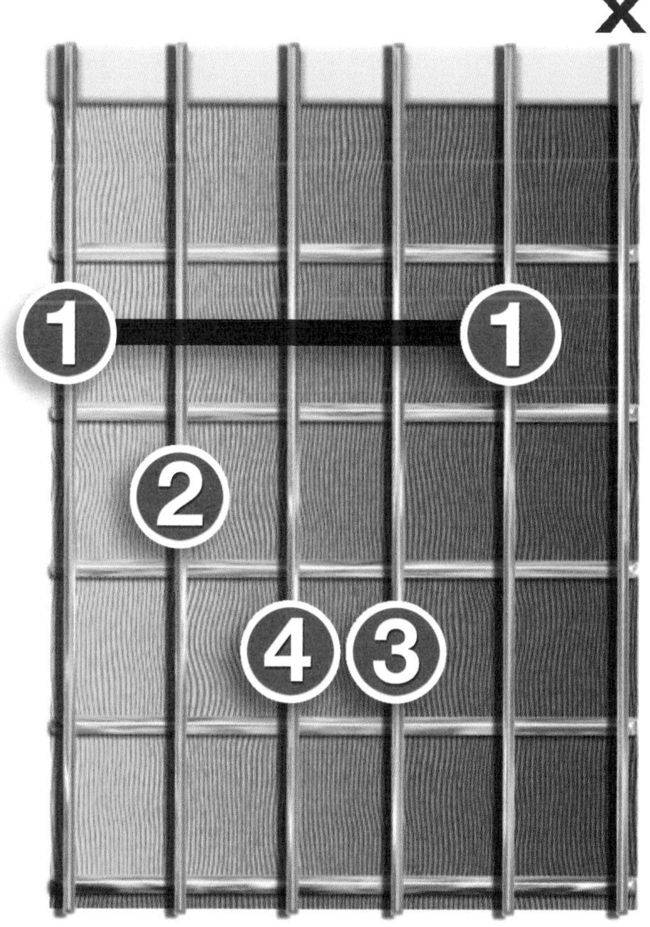


**Chord Spelling**

1st (B), ♭3rd (D), 5th (F♯)

**FREE ACCESS** on smartphones including iPhone & Android

Using any free QR code app, scan and **HEAR** the chord

# B+

## Augmented Triad

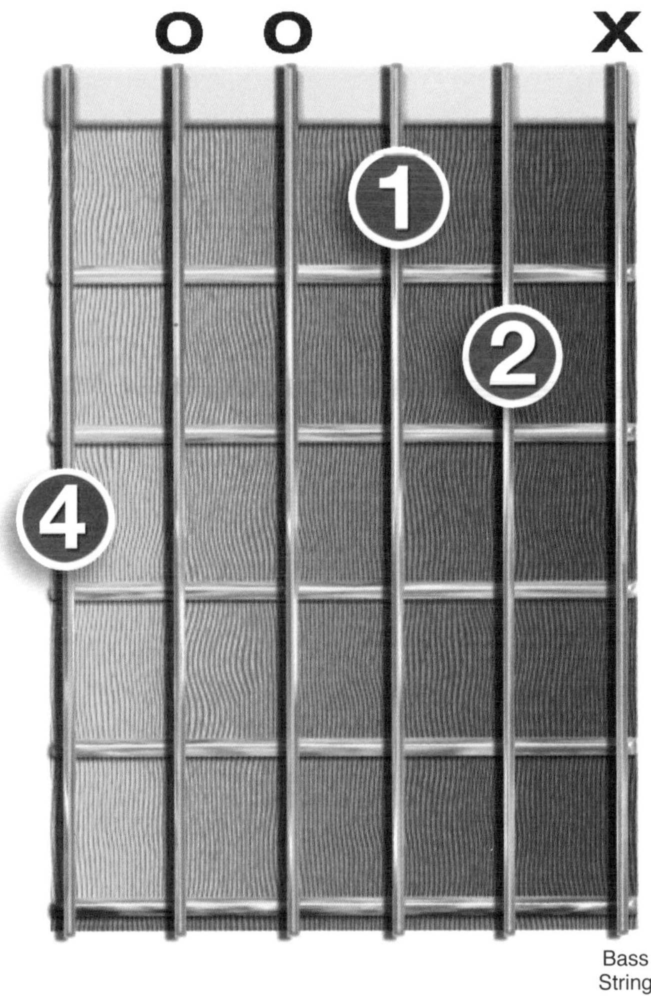


**Chord Spelling**

1st (B), 3rd (D♯), ♯5th (F𝄪)

**FREE ACCESS** on smartphones including iPhone & Android

Using any free QR code app, scan and **HEAR** the chord

# B°

## Diminished Triad

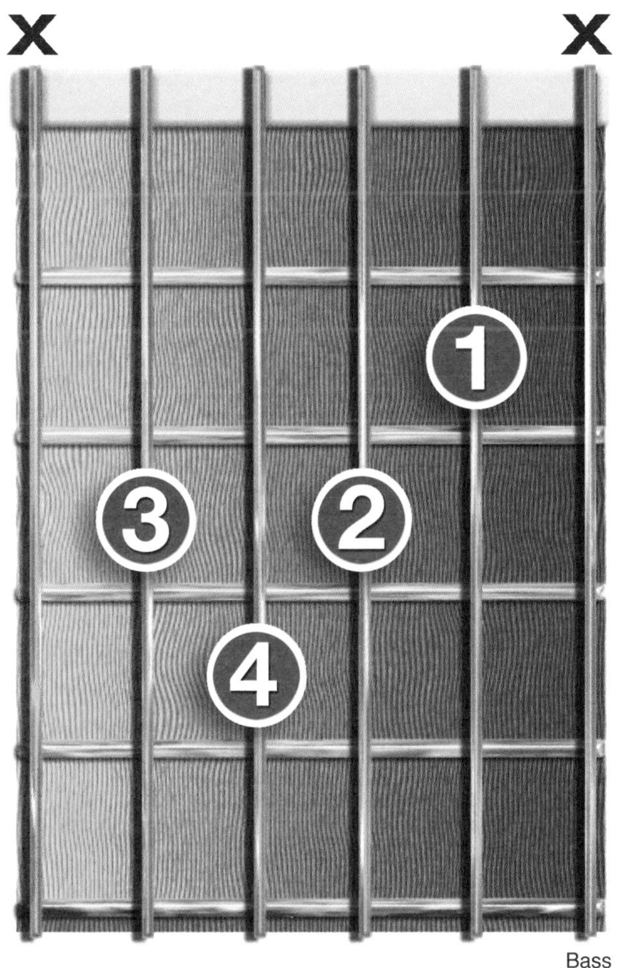


### Chord Spelling

1st (B), ♭3rd (D), ♭5th (F)

**FREE ACCESS** on smartphones including iPhone & Android

Using any free QR code app, scan and **HEAR** the chord

# Bsus2

## Suspended 2nd

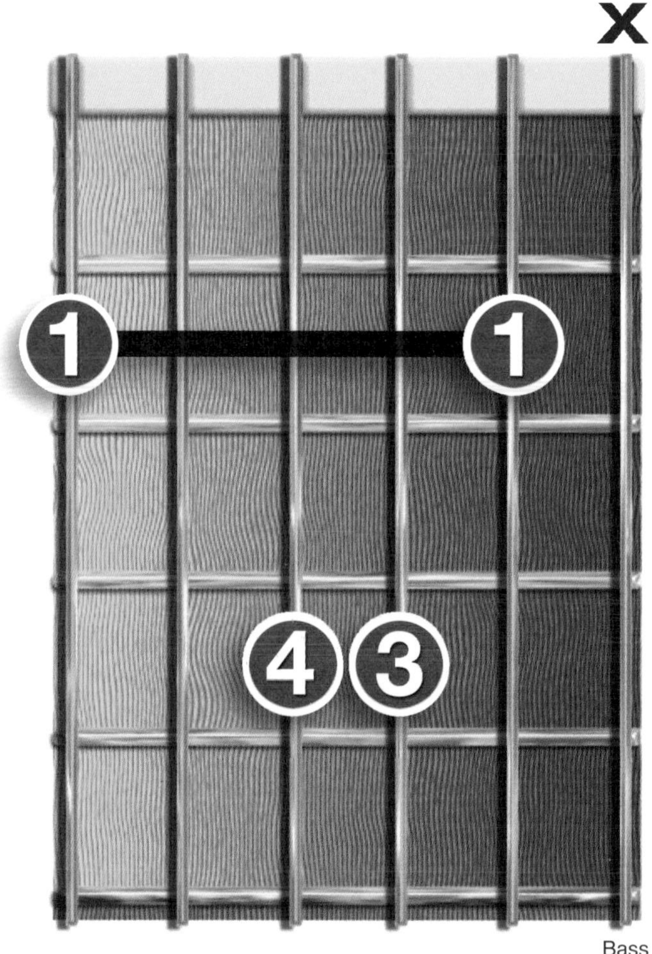


### Chord Spelling

1st (B), 2nd (C♯), 5th (F♯)

**FREE ACCESS** on smartphones including iPhone & Android

Using any free QR code app, scan and **HEAR** the chord

# Bsus4

## Suspended 4th

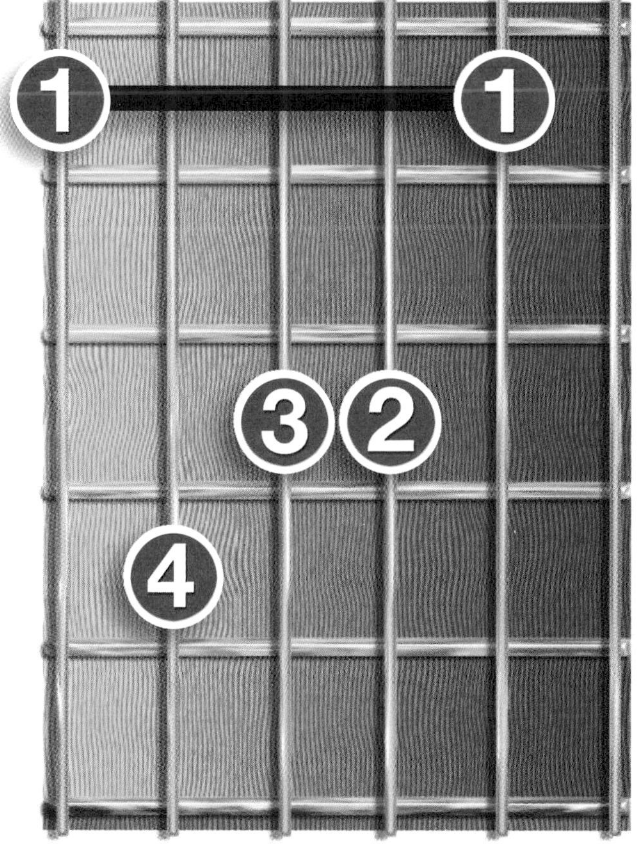


Bass String

**Chord Spelling**

1st (B), 4th (E), 5th (F♯)

B

**FREE ACCESS** on smartphones including iPhone & Android

Using any free QR code app, scan and **HEAR** the chord

# B5

## 5th (Power Chord)

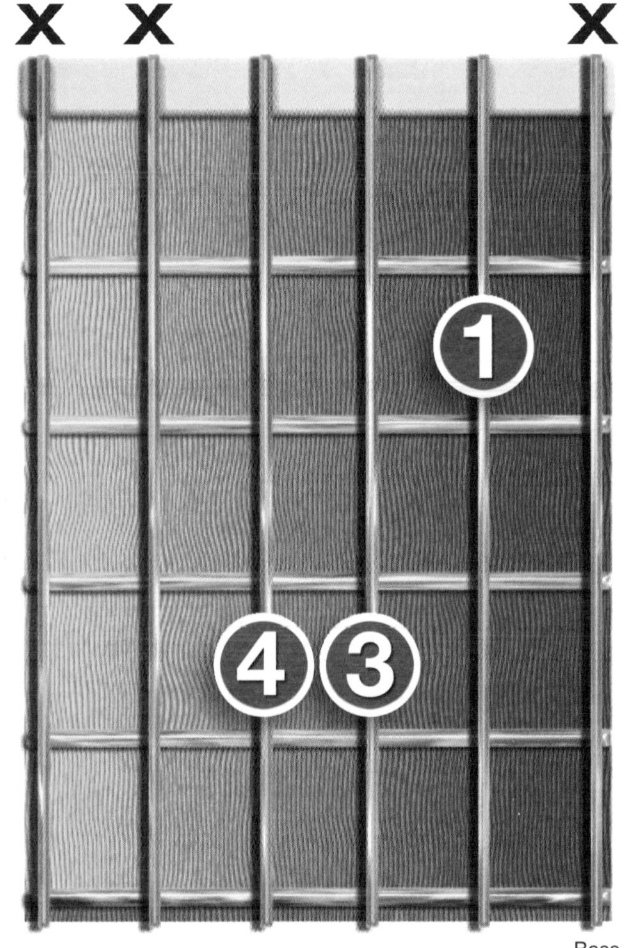


### Chord Spelling

1st (B), 5th (F♯)

**FREE ACCESS** on smartphones including iPhone & Android

Using any free QR code app, scan and **HEAR** the chord

# B6

## Major 6th

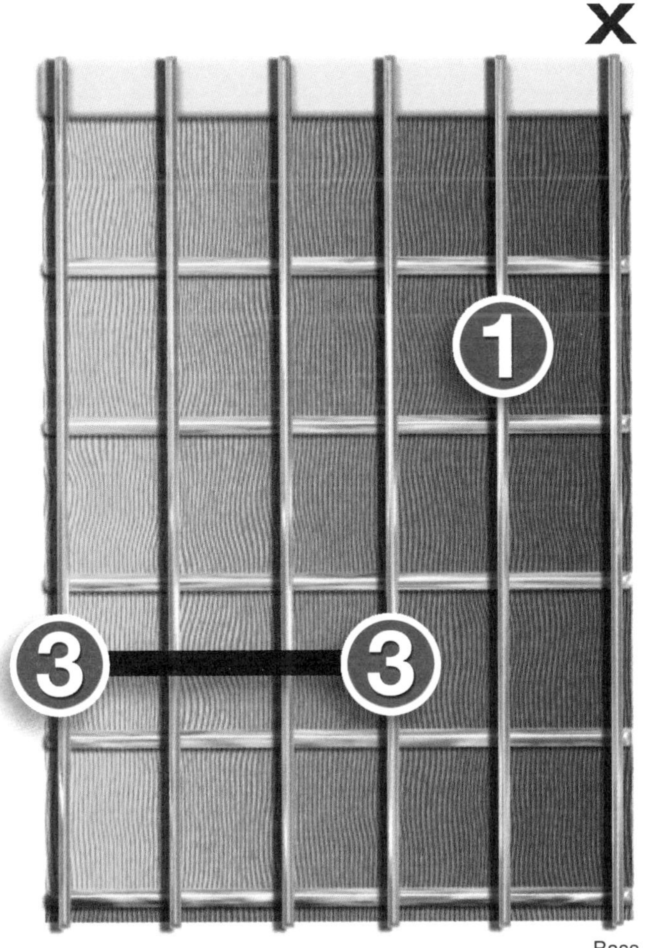


### Chord Spelling

1st (B), 3rd (D♯), 5th (F♯), 6th (G♯)

**FREE ACCESS** on smartphones including iPhone & Android

Using any free QR code app, scan and **HEAR** the chord

# Bm6

## Minor 6th

### Chord Spelling

1st (B), ♭3rd (D), 5th (F♯), 6th (G♯)

**FREE ACCESS** on smartphones including iPhone & Android

Using any free QR code app, scan and **HEAR** the chord

# Bmaj7

## Major 7th

### Chord Spelling

1st (B), 3rd (D♯), 5th (F♯), 7th (A♯)

**FREE ACCESS** on smartphones including iPhone & Android

Using any free QR code app, scan and **HEAR** the chord

# Bm7

## Minor 7th

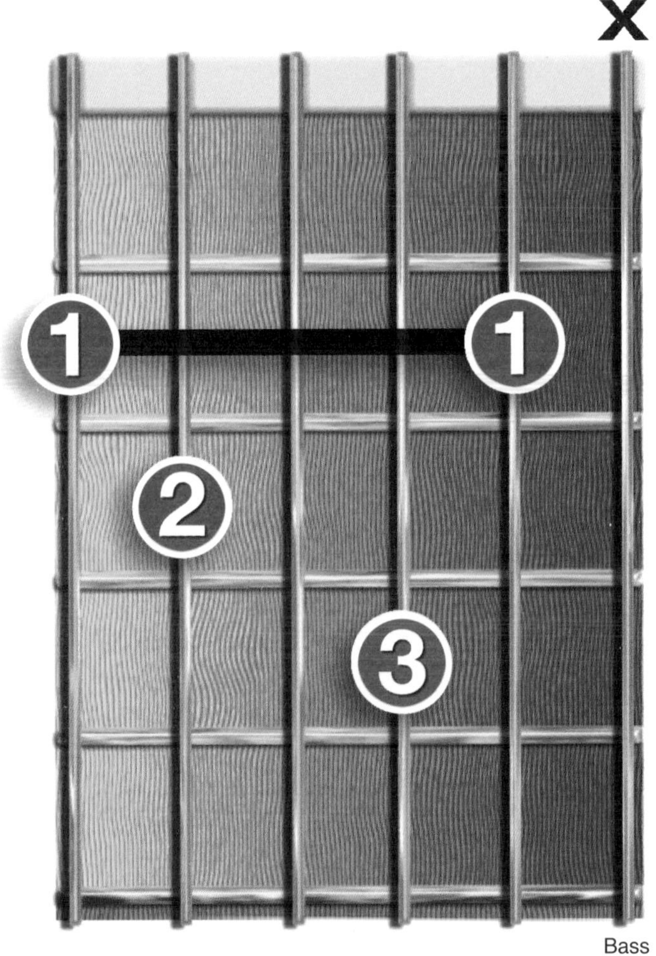


Bass String

**Chord Spelling**

1st (B), ♭3rd (D), 5th (F♯), ♭7th (A)

**FREE ACCESS** on smartphones including iPhone & Android

Using any free QR code app, scan and **HEAR** the chord

# B7

## Dominant 7th

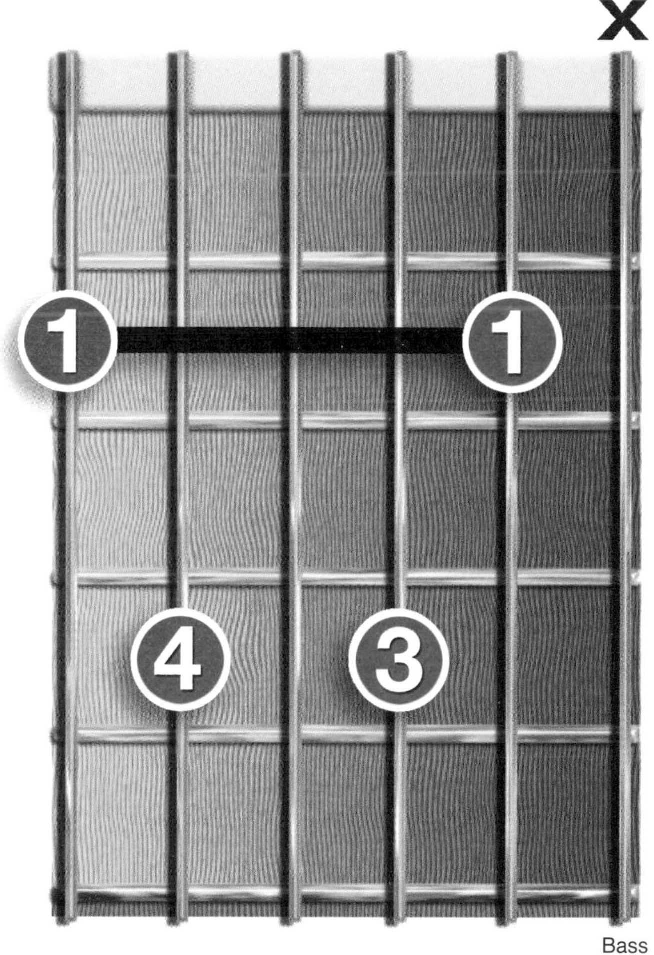


### Chord Spelling

1st (B), 3rd (D♯), 5th (F♯), ♭7th (A)

**FREE ACCESS** on smartphones including iPhone & Android

Using any free QR code app, scan and **HEAR** the chord

# B°7

## Diminished 7th

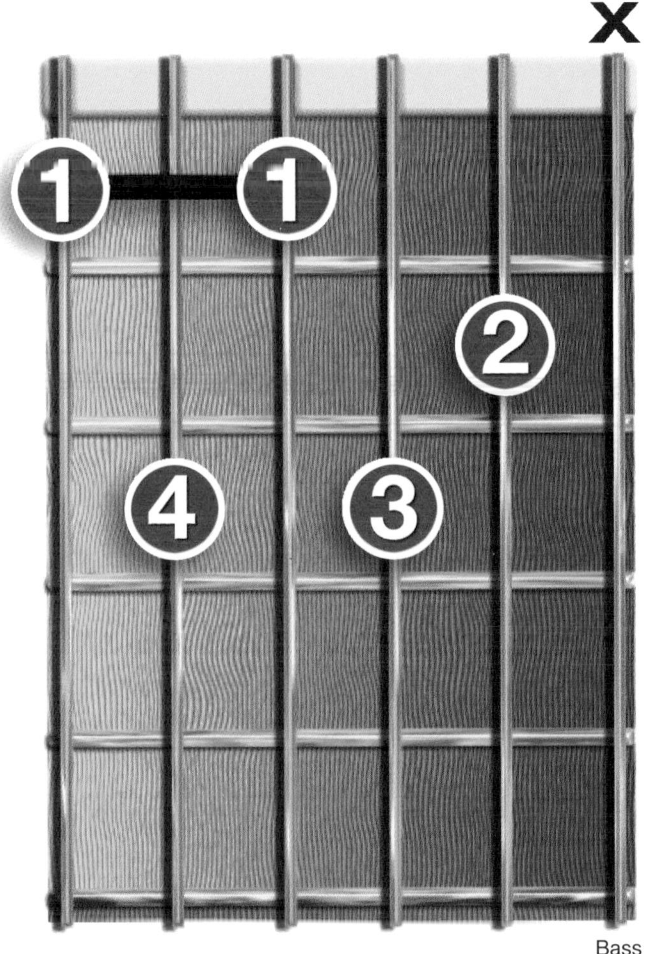


**Chord Spelling**

1st (B), ♭3rd (D), ♭5th (F), 𝄫7th (A♭)

**FREE ACCESS** on smartphones including iPhone & Android

Using any free QR code app, scan and **HEAR** the chord

# Bmaj9

## Major 9th

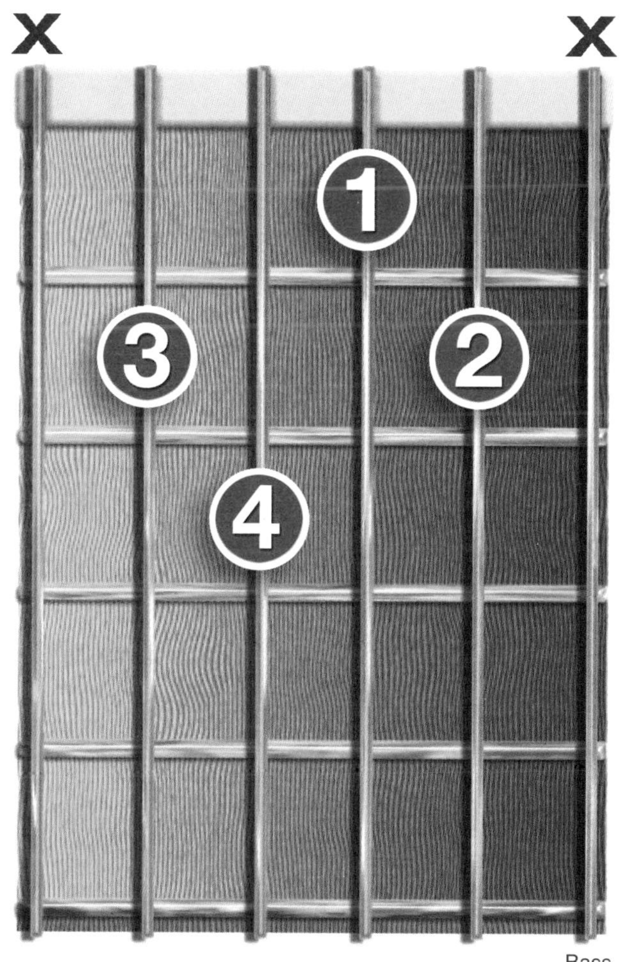


**Chord Spelling**

1st (B), 3rd (D♯), 5th (F♯), 7th (A♯), 9th (C♯)

**FREE ACCESS** on smartphones including iPhone & Android

Using any free QR code app, scan and **HEAR** the chord

# C

## Major

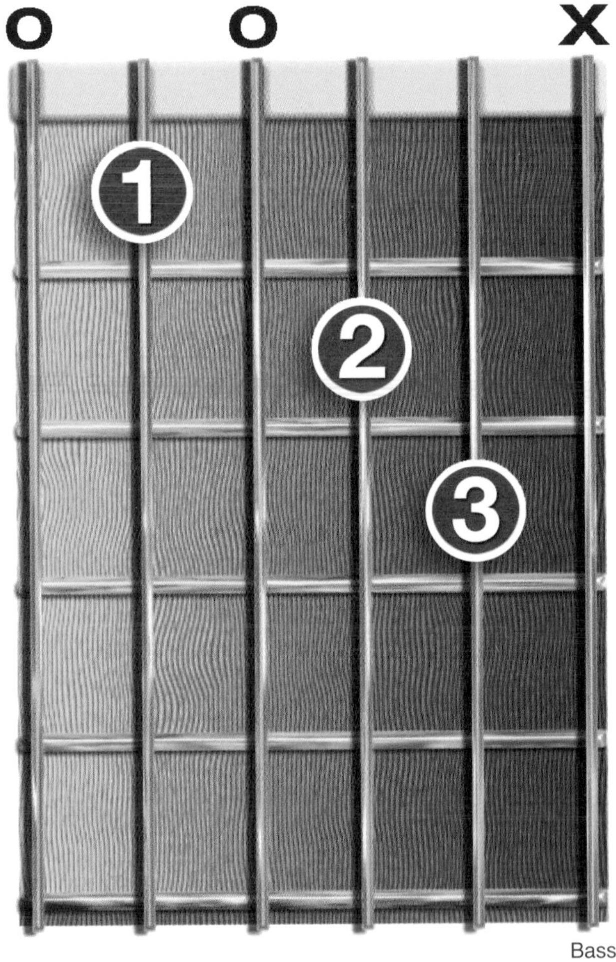


**Chord Spelling**

1st (C), 3rd (E), 5th (G)

**FREE ACCESS** on smartphones including iPhone & Android

Using any free QR code app, scan and **HEAR** the chord

# Cm
## Minor

3

Bass String

**Chord Spelling**

1st (C), ♭3rd (E♭), 5th (G)

**FREE ACCESS** on smartphones including iPhone & Android

Using any free QR code app, scan and **HEAR** the chord

# C+

## Augmented Triad

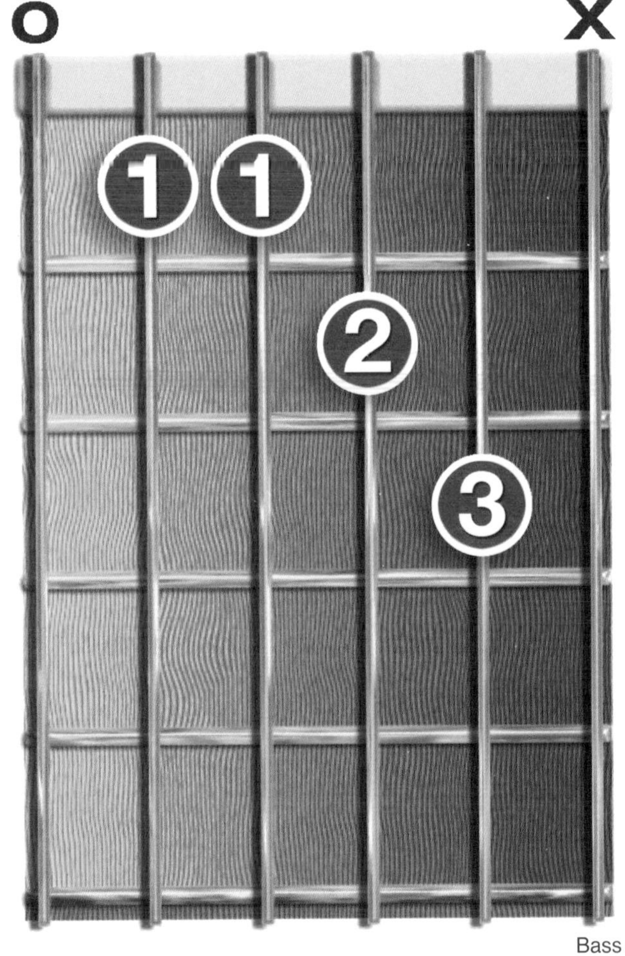


**Chord Spelling**

1st (C), 3rd (E), ♯5th (G♯)

**FREE ACCESS** on smartphones including iPhone & Android

Using any free QR code app, scan and **HEAR** the chord

# C°

## Diminished Triad

X X

3

1 3 2 4

Bass String

**Chord Spelling**

1st (C), ♭3rd (E♭), ♭5th (G♭)

**FREE ACCESS** on smartphones including iPhone & Android

Using any free QR code app, scan and **HEAR** the chord

A
A♯/B♭
B
C
C♯/D♭
D
D♯/E♭
E
F
F♯/G♭
G
G♯/A♭

# Csus2

## Suspended 2nd

**Chord Spelling**

1st (C), 2nd (D), 5th (G)

**FREE ACCESS** on smartphones including iPhone & Android

Using any free QR code app, scan and **HEAR** the chord

# Csus4

## Suspended 4th

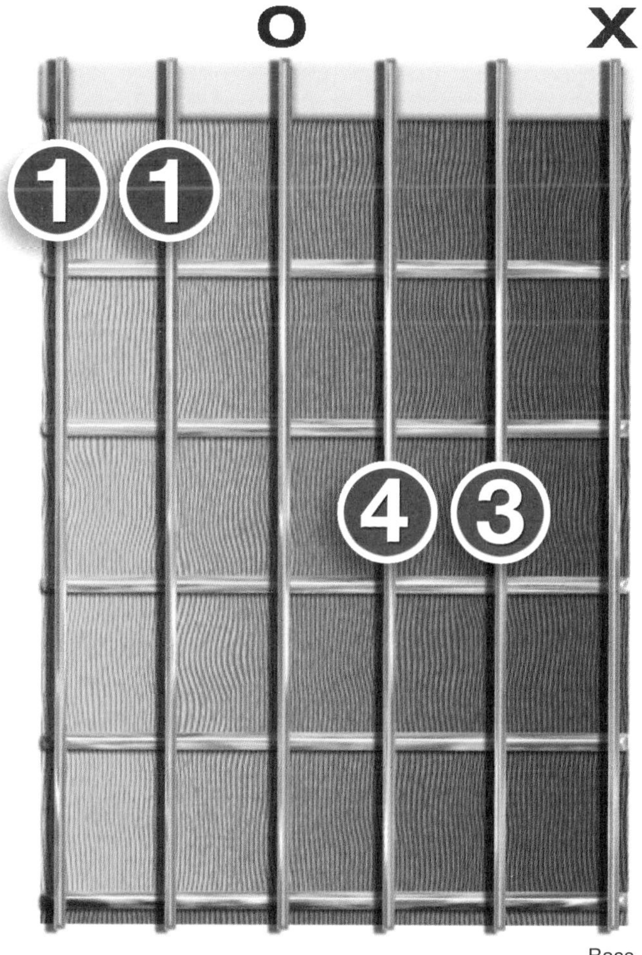


**Chord Spelling**

1st (C), 4th (F), 5th (G)

**FREE ACCESS** on smartphones including iPhone & Android

Using any free QR code app, scan and **HEAR** the chord

# C5

## 5th (Power Chord)

X

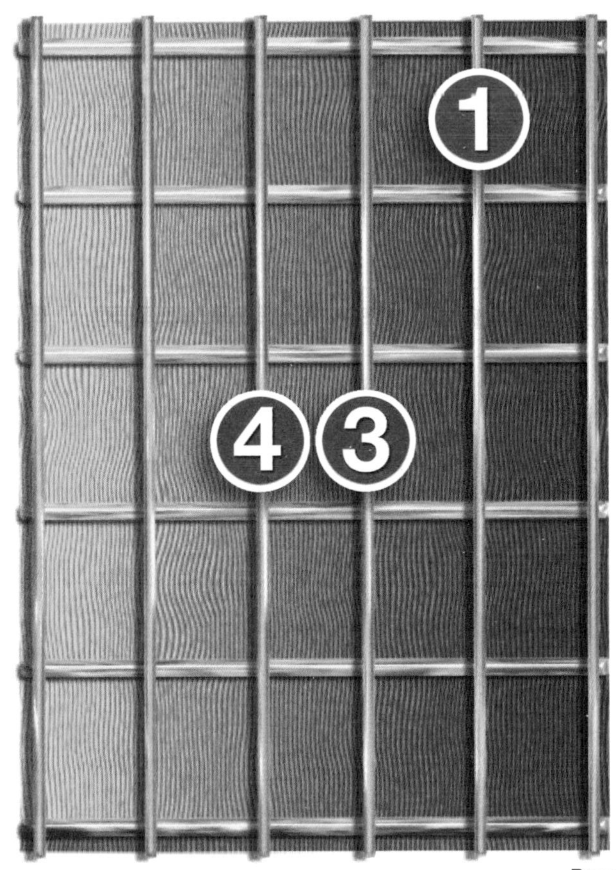


Bass String

**Chord Spelling**

1st (C), 5th (G)

**FREE ACCESS** on smartphones including iPhone & Android

Using any free QR code app, scan and **HEAR** the chord

# C6
## Major 6th

X

3

1

3 3

Bass String

**Chord Spelling**

1st (C), 3rd (E), 5th (G), 6th (A)

**FREE ACCESS** on smartphones including iPhone & Android

Using any free QR code app, scan and **HEAR** the chord

# Cm6

## Minor 6th

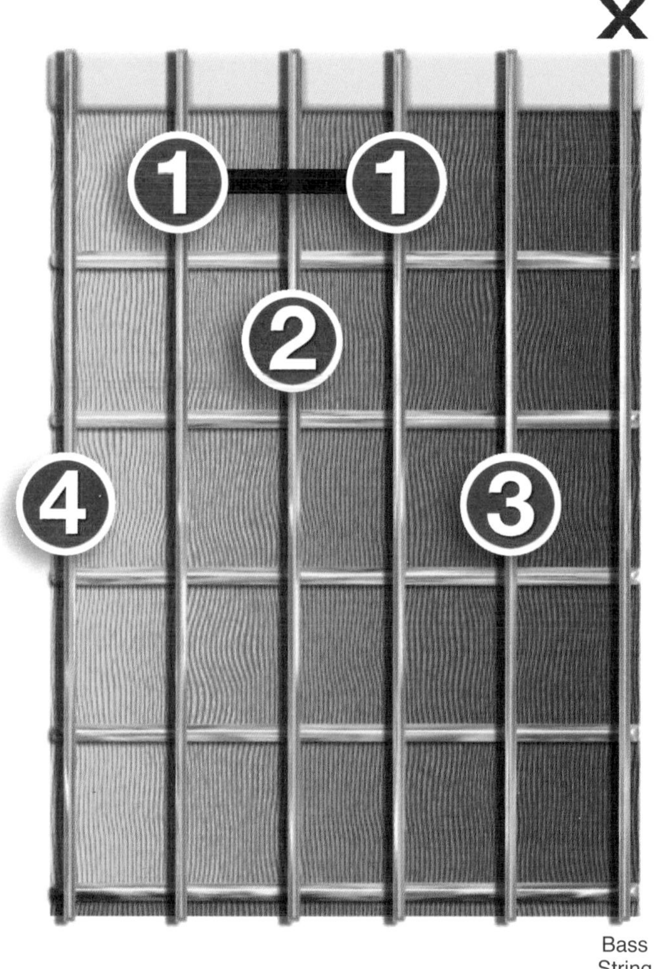


### Chord Spelling

1st (C), ♭3rd (E♭), 5th (G), 6th (A)

**FREE ACCESS** on smartphones including iPhone & Android

Using any free QR code app, scan and **HEAR** the chord

# Cmaj7

## Major 7th

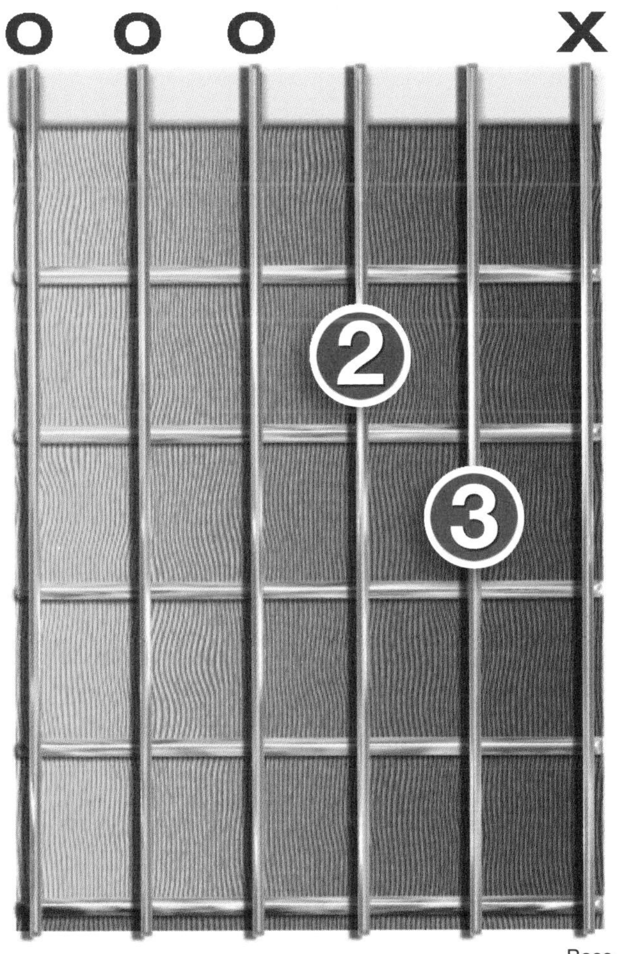


### Chord Spelling

1st (C), 3rd (E), 5th (G), 7th (B)

**FREE ACCESS** on smartphones including iPhone & Android

Using any free QR code app, scan and **HEAR** the chord

# Cm7

## Minor 7th

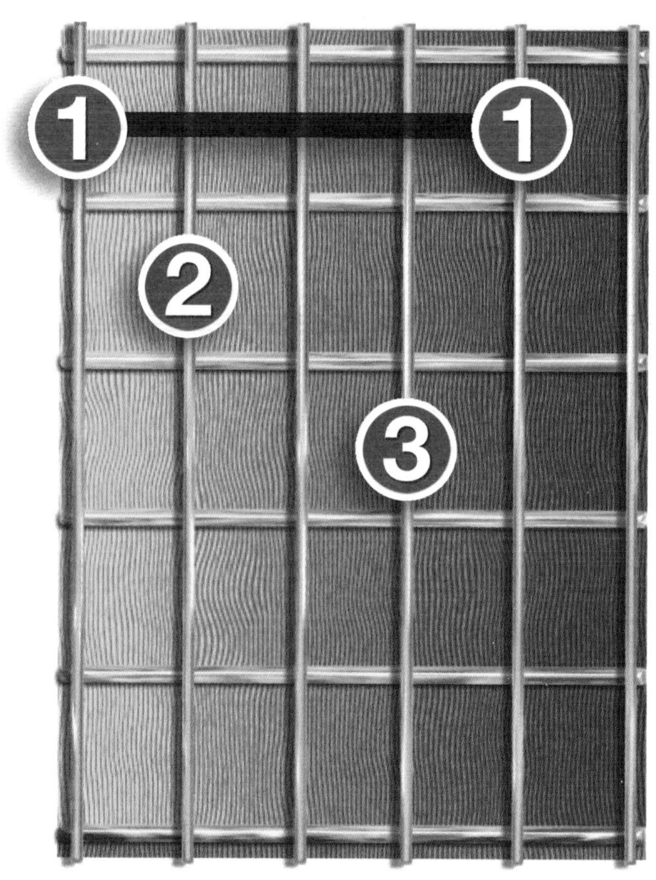


### Chord Spelling

1st (C), ♭3rd (E♭), 5th (G), ♭7th (B♭)

**FREE ACCESS** on smartphones including iPhone & Android

Using any free QR code app, scan and **HEAR** the chord

# C7

## Dominant 7th

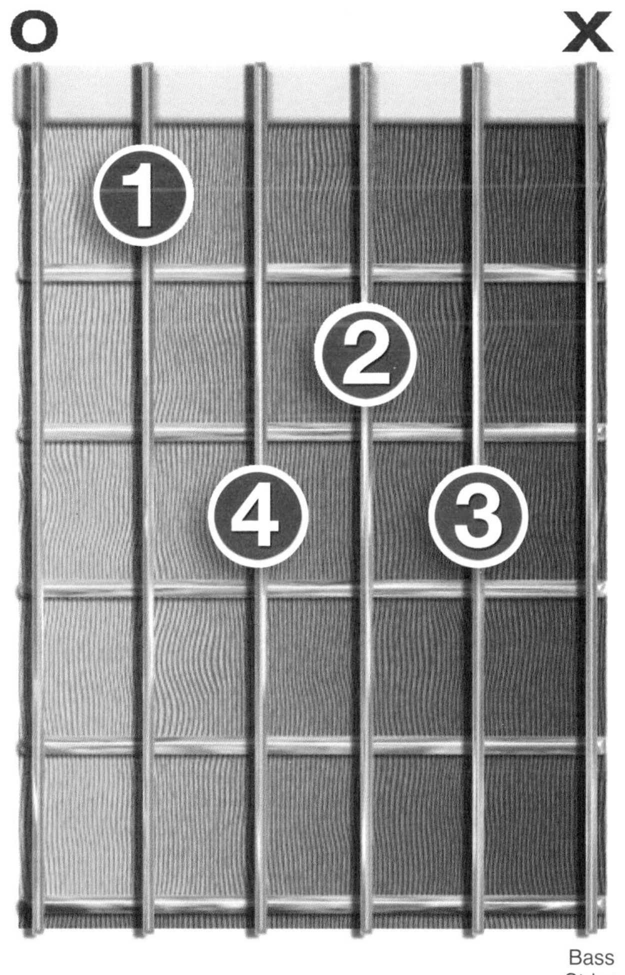


### Chord Spelling

1st (C), 3rd (E), 5th (G), ♭7th (B♭)

**FREE ACCESS** on smartphones including iPhone & Android

Using any free QR code app, scan and **HEAR** the chord

# C°7

## Diminished 7th

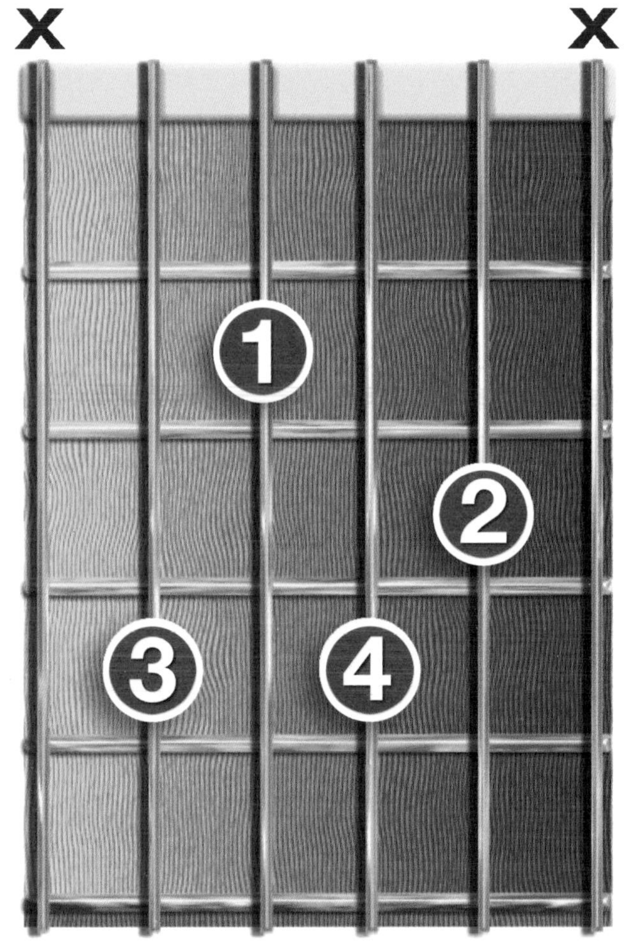


**Chord Spelling**

1st (C), ♭3rd (E♭), ♭5th (G♭), 𝄫7th (B𝄫)

**FREE ACCESS** on smartphones including iPhone & Android

Using any free QR code app, scan and **HEAR** the chord

# Cmaj9

## Major 9th

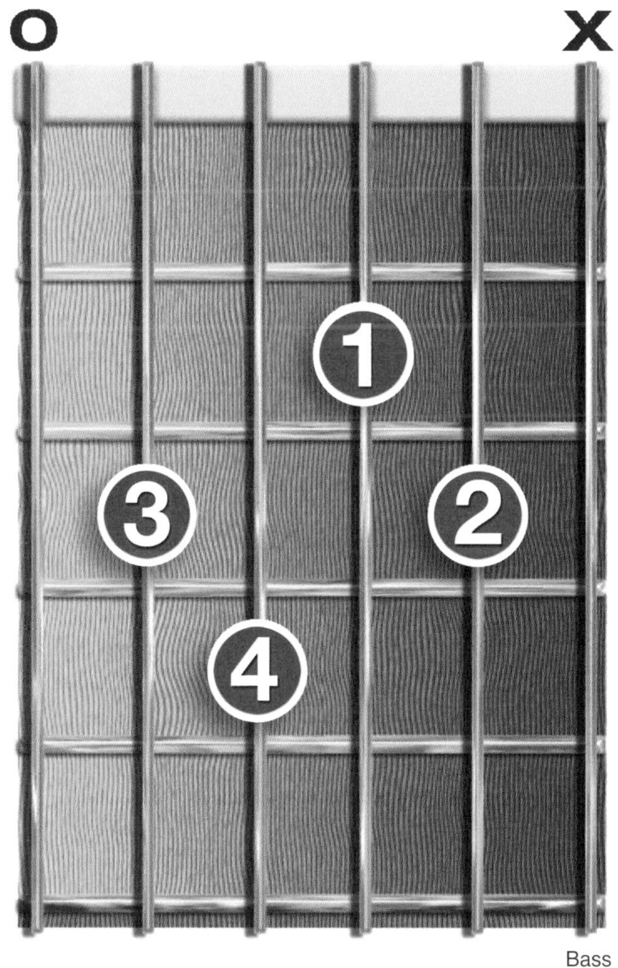


**Chord Spelling**

1st (C), 3rd (E), 5th (G), 7th (B), 9th (D)

**FREE ACCESS** on smartphones including iPhone & Android

Using any free QR code app, scan and **HEAR** the chord

# C♯/D♭
## Major

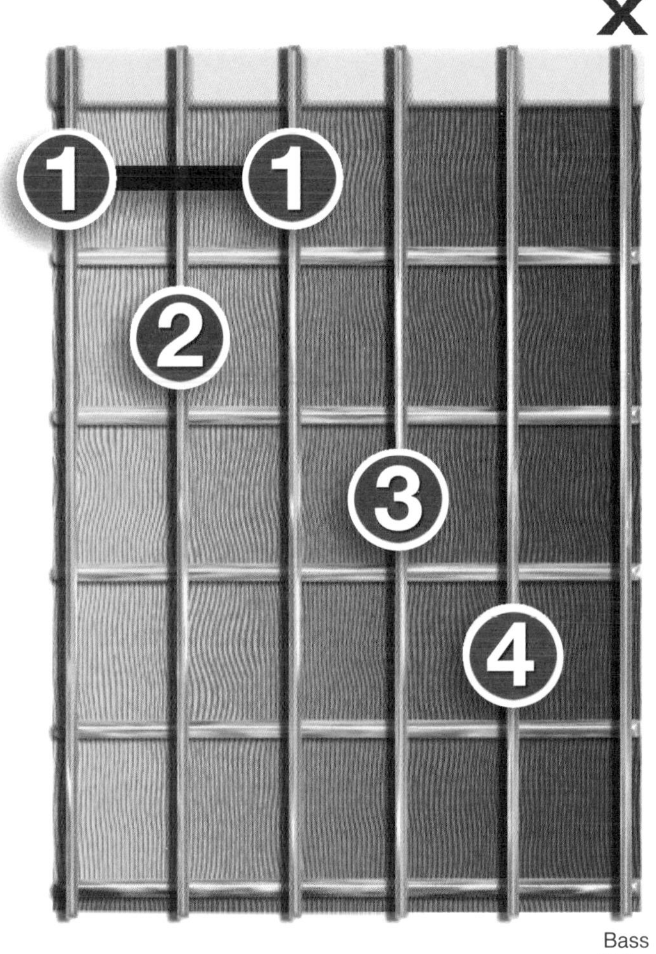


### Chord Spelling

1st (C♯), 3rd (E♯), 5th (G♯)

**FREE ACCESS** on smartphones including iPhone & Android

Using any free QR code app, scan and **HEAR** the chord

# C♯/D♭m
## Minor

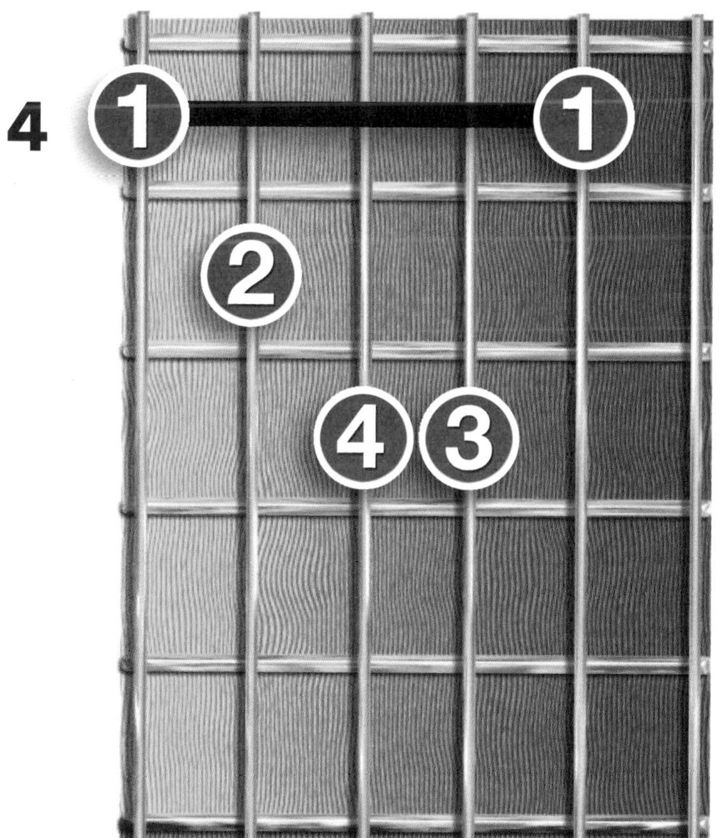


Bass
String

### Chord Spelling

1st (C♯), ♭3rd (E), 5th (G♯)

**FREE ACCESS** on smartphones including iPhone & Android

Using any free QR code app, scan and **HEAR** the chord

# C♯/D♭+

## Augmented Triad

X X

2

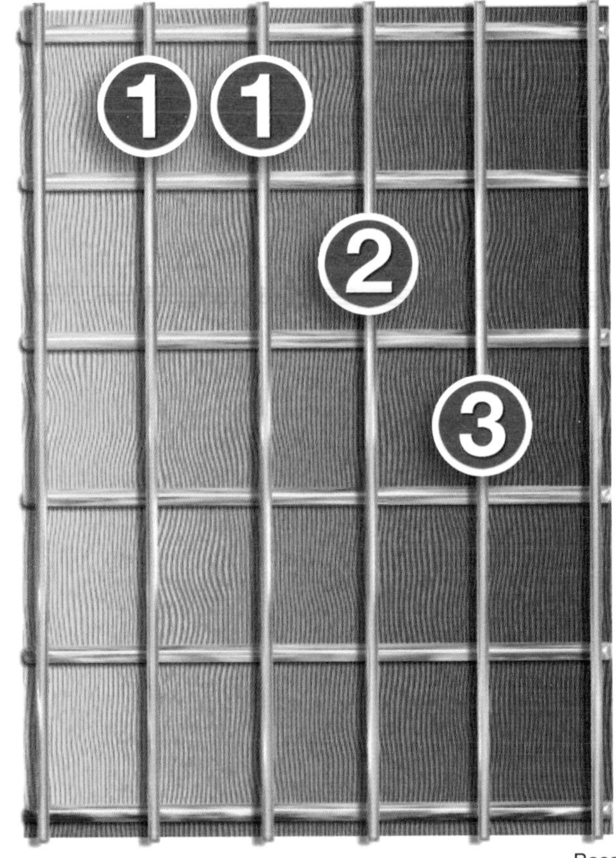


Bass String

**Chord Spelling**

1st (C♯), 3rd (E♯), ♯5th (G𝄪)

**FREE ACCESS** on smartphones including iPhone & Android

Using any free QR code app, scan and **HEAR** the chord

# C♯/D♭°

## Diminished Triad

**Chord Spelling**

1st (C♯), ♭3rd (E), ♭5th (G)

**FREE ACCESS** on smartphones including iPhone & Android

Using any free QR code app, scan and **HEAR** the chord

C♯/D♭

# C♯/D♭sus2

## Suspended 2nd

**Chord Spelling**

1st (C♯), 2nd (D♯), 5th (G♯)

**FREE ACCESS** on smartphones including iPhone & Android

Using any free QR code app, scan and **HEAR** the chord

# C♯/D♭sus4

## Suspended 4th

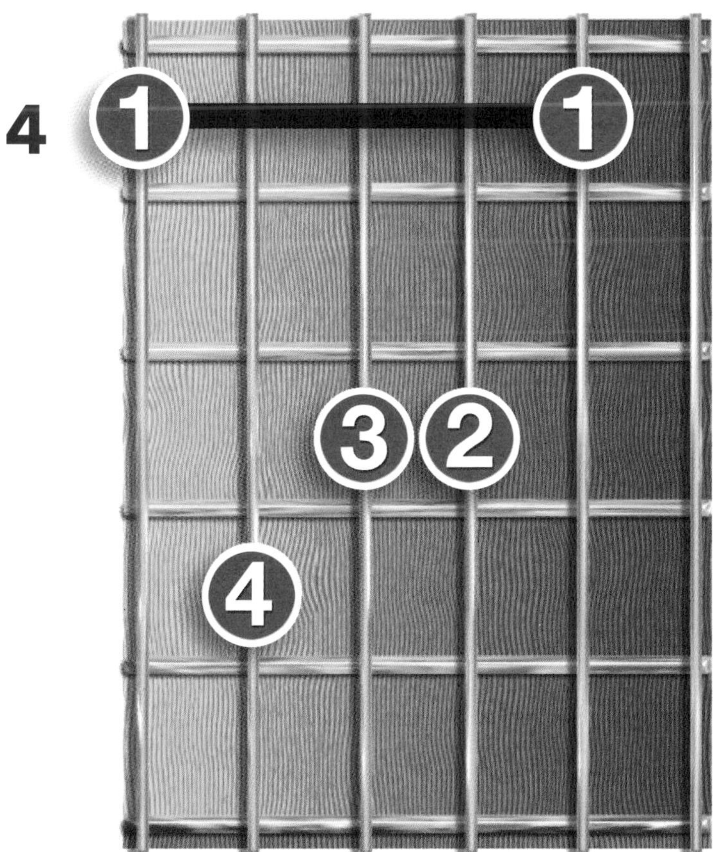


Bass String

**Chord Spelling**

1st (C♯), 4th (F♯), 5th (G♯)

**FREE ACCESS** on smartphones including iPhone & Android

Using any free QR code app, scan and **HEAR** the chord

# C♯/D♭5

## 5th (Power Chord)

4

Bass String

**Chord Spelling**

1st (C♯), 5th (G♯)

**FREE ACCESS** on smartphones including iPhone & Android

Using any free QR code app, scan and **HEAR** the chord

# C♯/D♭6
## Major 6th

4

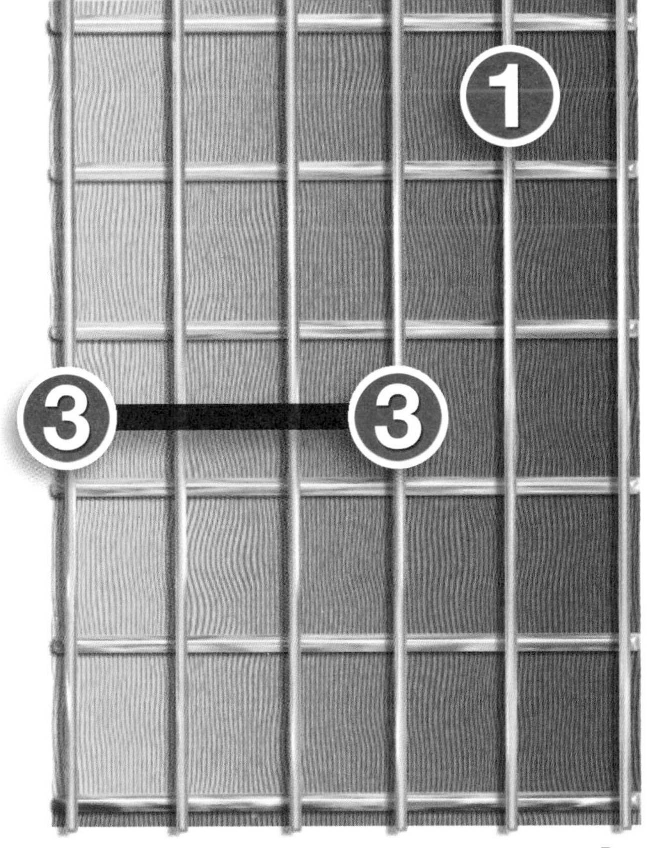


Bass String

**Chord Spelling**

1st (C♯), 3rd (E♯), 5th (G♯), 6th (A♯)

**FREE ACCESS** on smartphones including iPhone & Android

Using any free QR code app, scan and **HEAR** the chord

C♯/D♭

# C♯/D♭m6
## Minor 6th

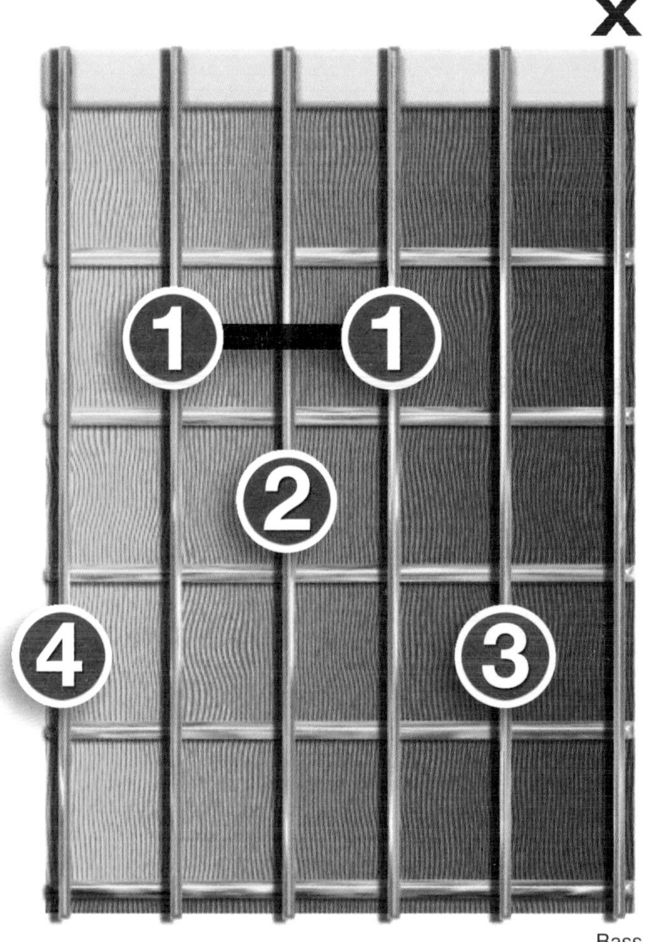


**Chord Spelling**

1st (C♯), ♭3rd (E), 5th (G♯), 6th (A♯)

**FREE ACCESS** on smartphones including iPhone & Android

Using any free QR code app, scan and **HEAR** the chord

# C♯/D♭maj7

## Major 7th

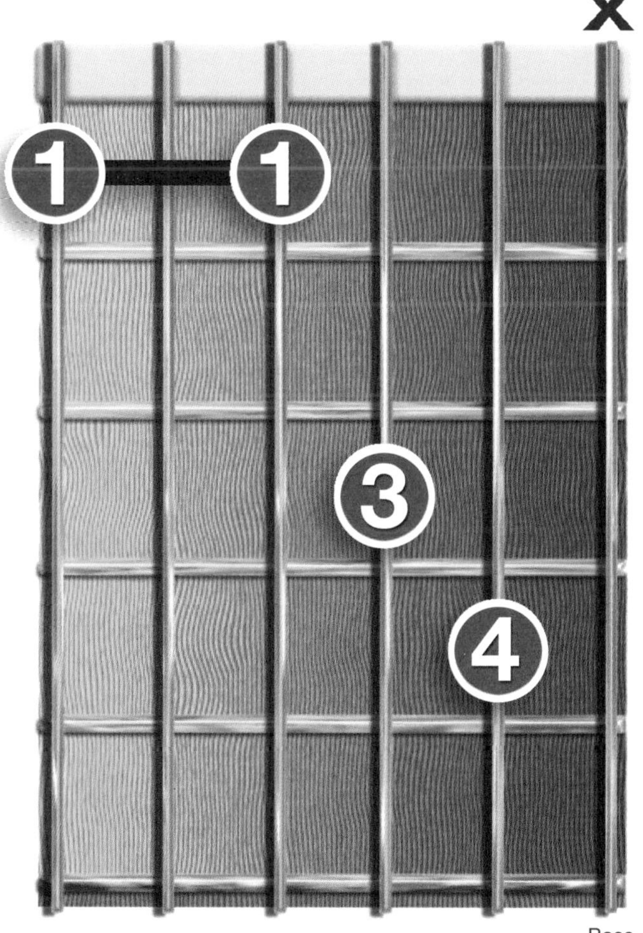


### Chord Spelling

1st (C♯), 3rd (E♯), 5th (G♯), 7th (B♯)

**FREE ACCESS** on smartphones including iPhone & Android

Using any free QR code app, scan and **HEAR** the chord

# C♯/D♭m7

## Minor 7th

### Chord Spelling

1st (C♯), ♭3rd (E), 5th (G♯), ♭7th (B)

**FREE ACCESS** on smartphones including iPhone & Android

Using any free QR code app, scan and **HEAR** the chord

# C♯/D♭7

## Dominant 7th

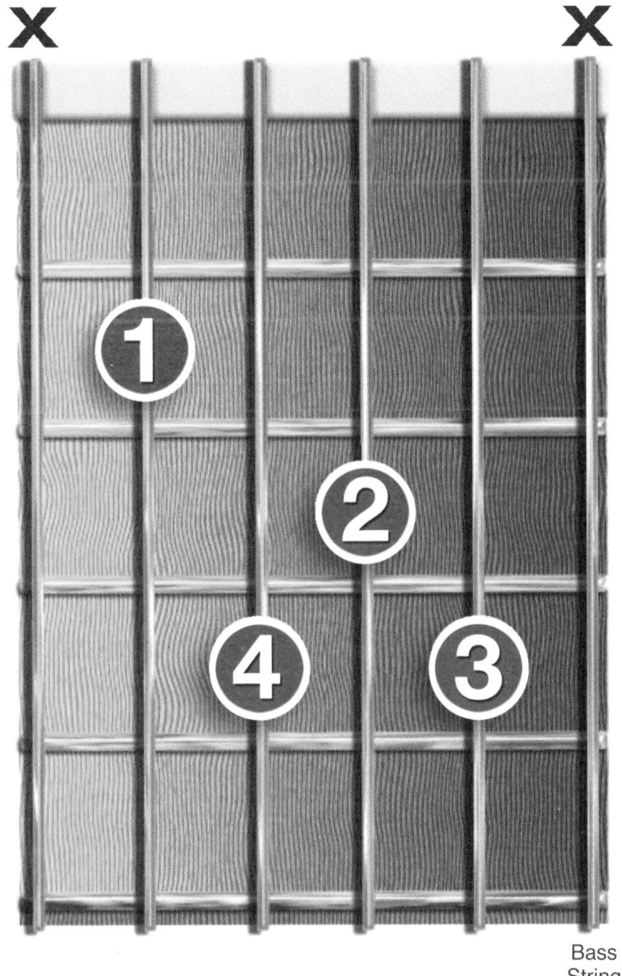


**Chord Spelling**

1st (C♯), 3rd (E♯), 5th (G♯), ♭7th (B)

**FREE ACCESS** on smartphones including iPhone & Android

Using any free QR code app, scan and **HEAR** the chord

# C♯/D♭°7

## Diminished 7th

3

Bass String

### Chord Spelling

1st (C♯), ♭3rd (E), ♭5th (G), 𝄫7th (B♭)

**FREE ACCESS** on smartphones including iPhone & Android

Using any free QR code app, scan and **HEAR** the chord

# C♯/D♭maj9

## Major 9th

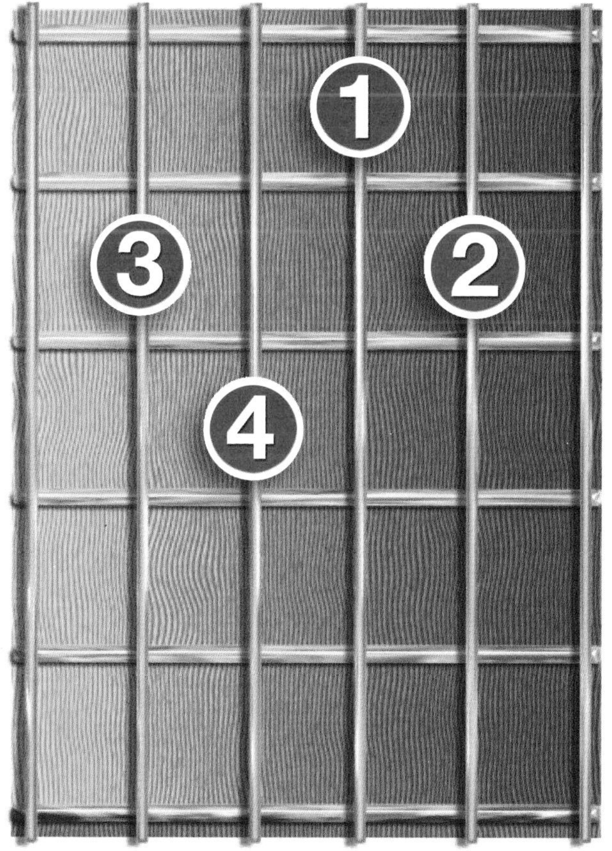


### Chord Spelling

1st (C♯), 3rd (E♯), 5th (G♯), 7th (B♯), 9th (D♯)

**FREE ACCESS** on smartphones including iPhone & Android

Using any free QR code app, scan and **HEAR** the chord

# D
## Major

### Chord Spelling

1st (D), 3rd (F♯), 5th (A)

**FREE ACCESS** on smartphones including iPhone & Android

Using any free QR code app, scan and **HEAR** the chord

# Dm

## Minor

**Chord Spelling**

1st (D), ♭3rd (F), 5th (A)

**FREE ACCESS** on smartphones including iPhone & Android

Using any free QR code app, scan and **HEAR** the chord

# D+

## Augmented Triad

3

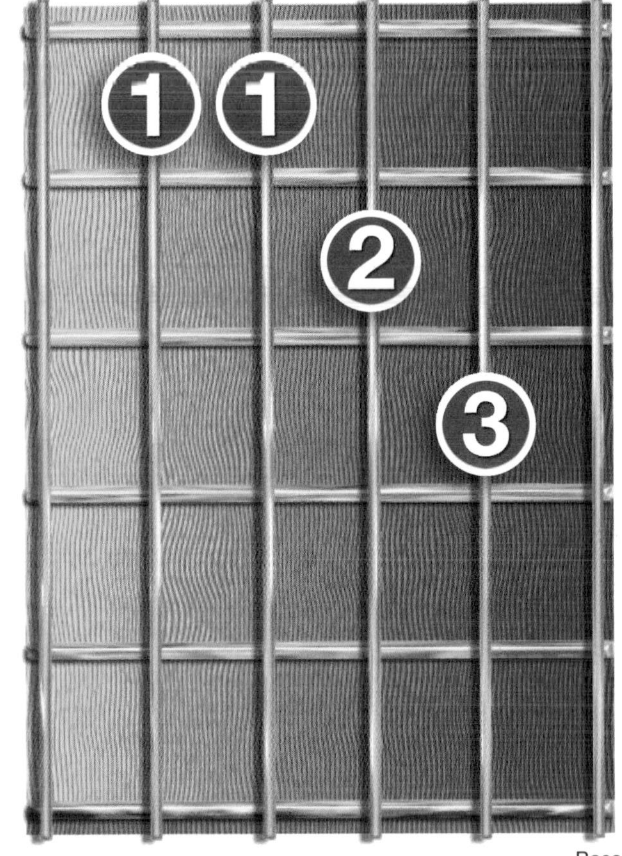


Bass String

**Chord Spelling**

1st (D), 3rd (F♯), ♯5th (A♯)

**FREE ACCESS** on smartphones including iPhone & Android

Using any free QR code app, scan and **HEAR** the chord

# D°

## Diminished Triad

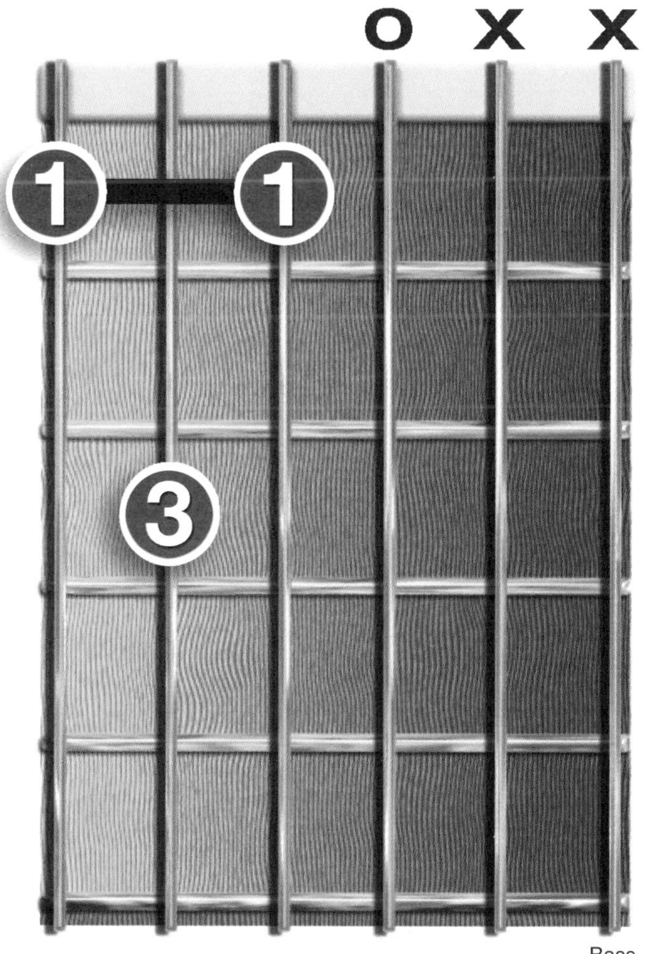


**Chord Spelling**

1st (D), ♭3rd (F), ♭5th (A♭)

**FREE ACCESS** on smartphones including iPhone & Android

Using any free QR code app, scan and **HEAR** the chord

# Dsus2

## Suspended 2nd

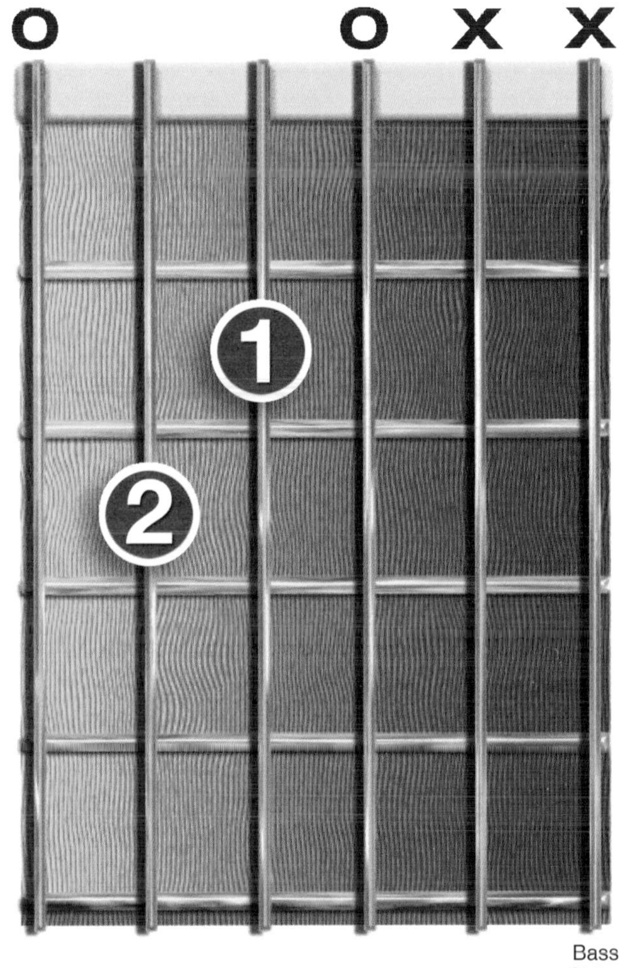


**Chord Spelling**

1st (D), 2nd (E), 5th (A)

**FREE ACCESS** on smartphones including iPhone & Android

Using any free QR code app, scan and **HEAR** the chord

# Dsus4

## Suspended 4th

**Chord Spelling**

1st (D), 4th (G), 5th (A)

**FREE ACCESS** on smartphones including iPhone & Android

Using any free QR code app, scan and **HEAR** the chord

# D5

## 5th (Power Chord)

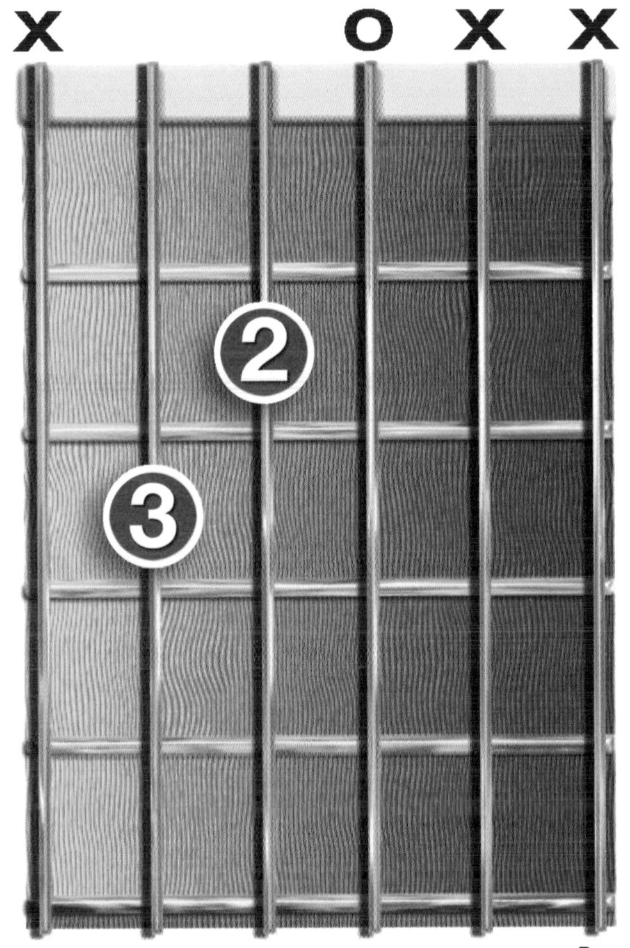


### Chord Spelling

1st (D), 5th (A)

**FREE ACCESS** on smartphones including iPhone & Android

Using any free QR code app, scan and **HEAR** the chord

# D6

## Major 6th

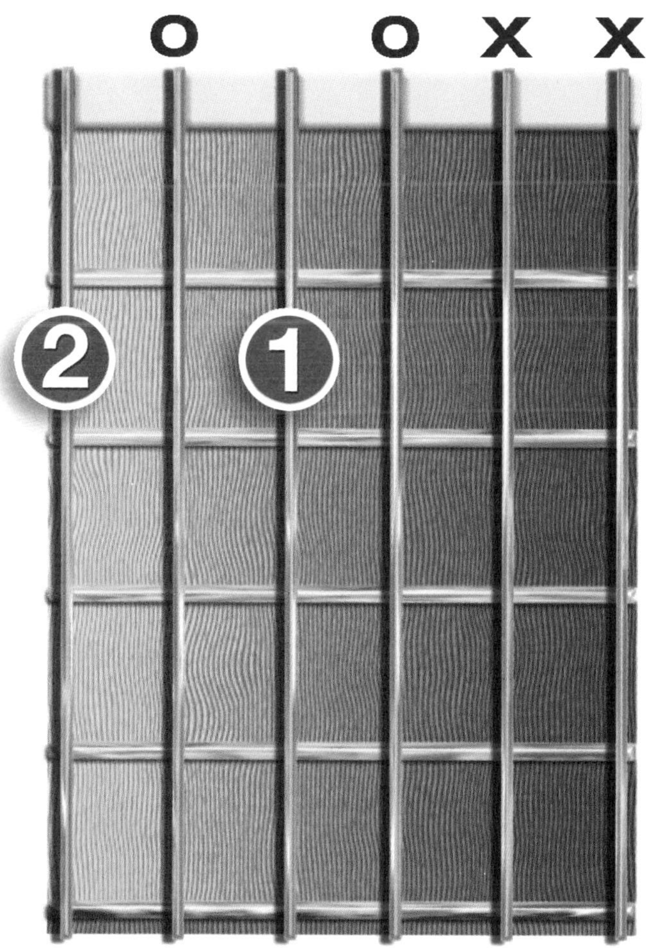


**Chord Spelling**

1st (D), 3rd (F♯), 5th (A), 6th (B)

**FREE ACCESS** on smartphones including iPhone & Android

Using any free QR code app, scan and **HEAR** the chord

# Dm6

## Minor 6th

**Chord Spelling**

1st (D), ♭3rd (F), 5th (A), 6th (B)

**FREE ACCESS** on smartphones including iPhone & Android

Using any free QR code app, scan and **HEAR** the chord

# Dmaj7

## Major 7th

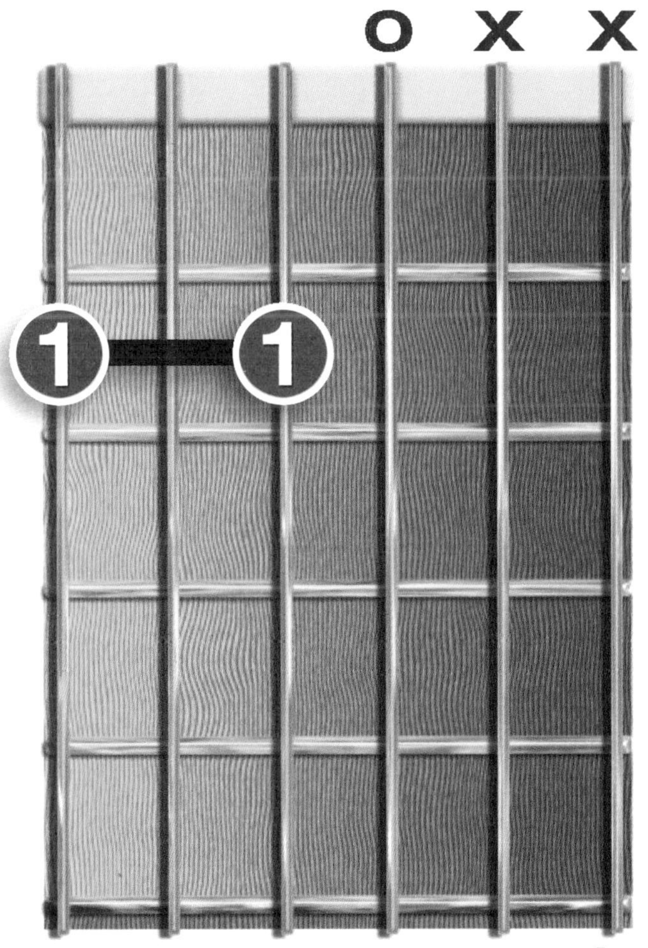


**Chord Spelling**

1st (D), 3rd (F♯), 5th (A), 7th (C♯)

**FREE ACCESS** on smartphones including iPhone & Android

Using any free QR code app, scan and **HEAR** the chord

D

# Dm7

## Minor 7th

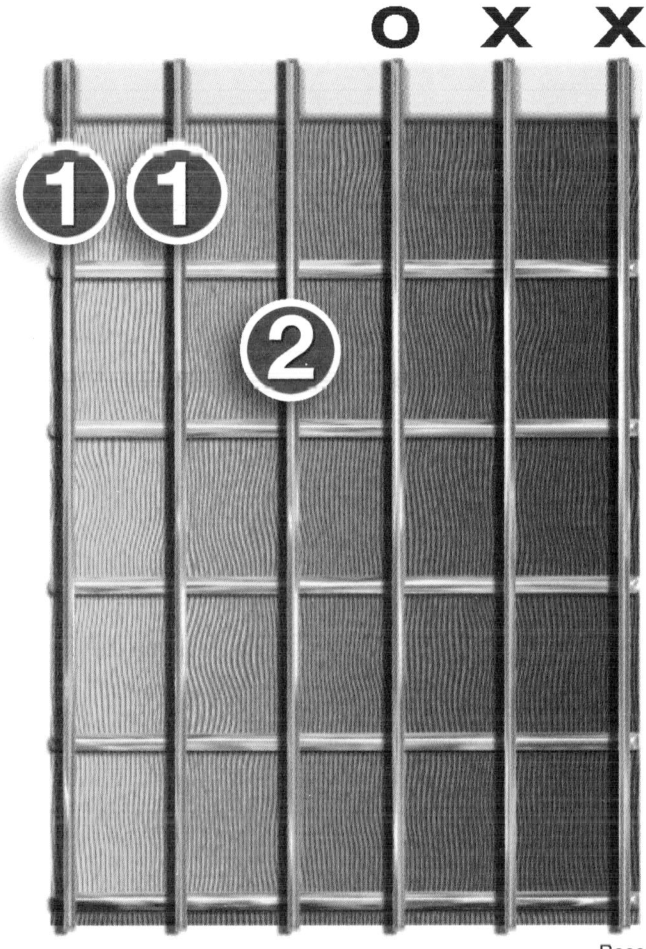


### Chord Spelling

1st (D), ♭3rd (F), 5th (A), ♭7th (C)

**FREE ACCESS** on smartphones including iPhone & Android

Using any free QR code app, scan and **HEAR** the chord

# D7

## Dominant 7th

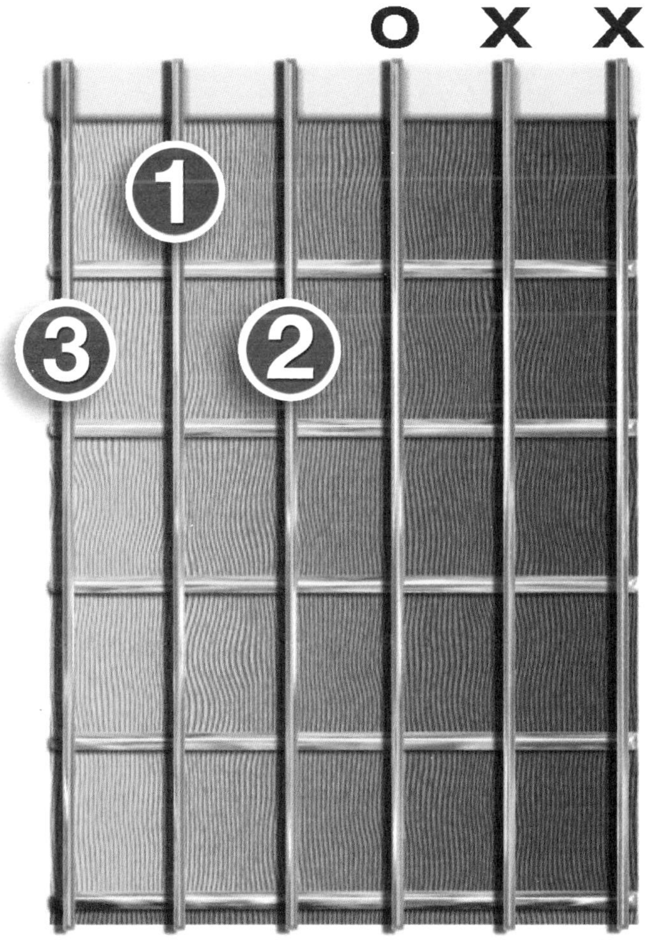


### Chord Spelling

1st (D), 3rd (F♯), 5th (A), ♭7th (C)

**FREE ACCESS** on smartphones including iPhone & Android

Using any free QR code app, scan and **HEAR** the chord

# D°7

## Diminished 7th

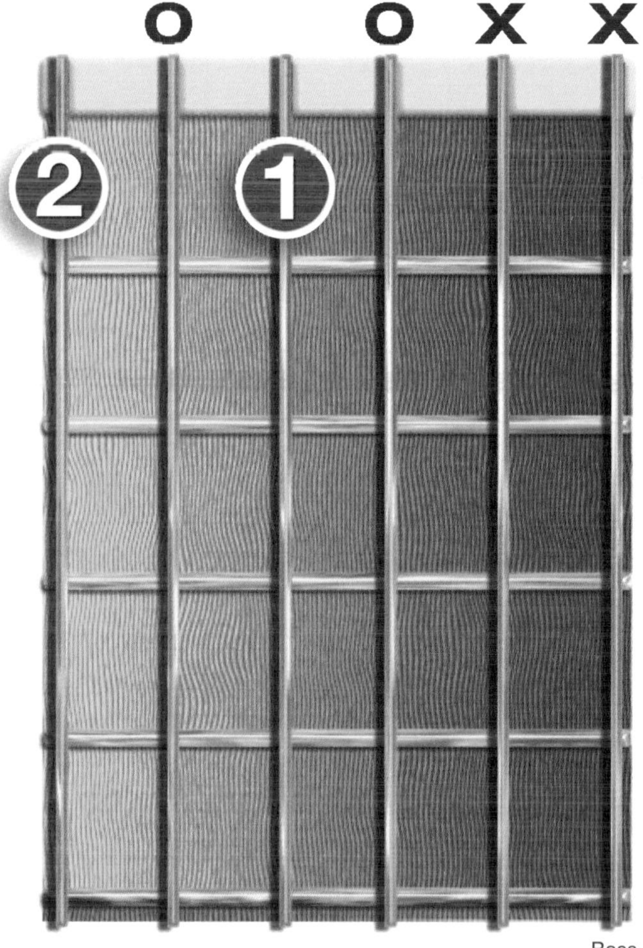


**Chord Spelling**

1st (D), ♭3rd (F), ♭5th (A♭), 𝄫7th (B)

**FREE ACCESS** on smartphones including iPhone & Android

Using any free QR code app, scan and **HEAR** the chord

# Dmaj9

## Major 9th

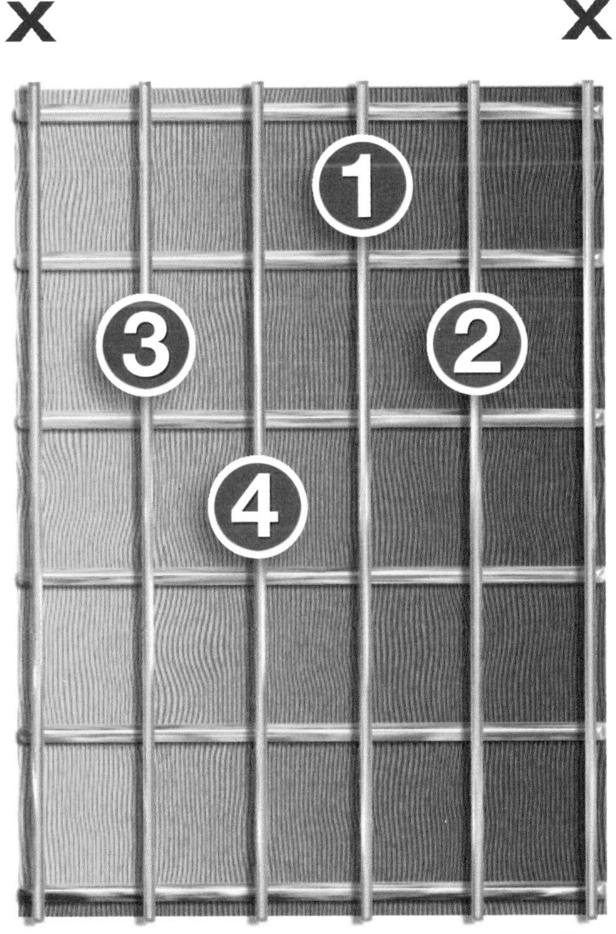


**Chord Spelling**

1st (D), 3rd (F♯), 5th (A), 7th (C♯), 9th (E)

**FREE ACCESS** on smartphones including iPhone & Android

Using any free QR code app, scan and **HEAR** the chord

A
A♯/B♭
B
C
C♯/D♭
D
D♯/E♭
E
F
F♯/G♭
G
G♯/A♭

# D♯/E♭
## Major

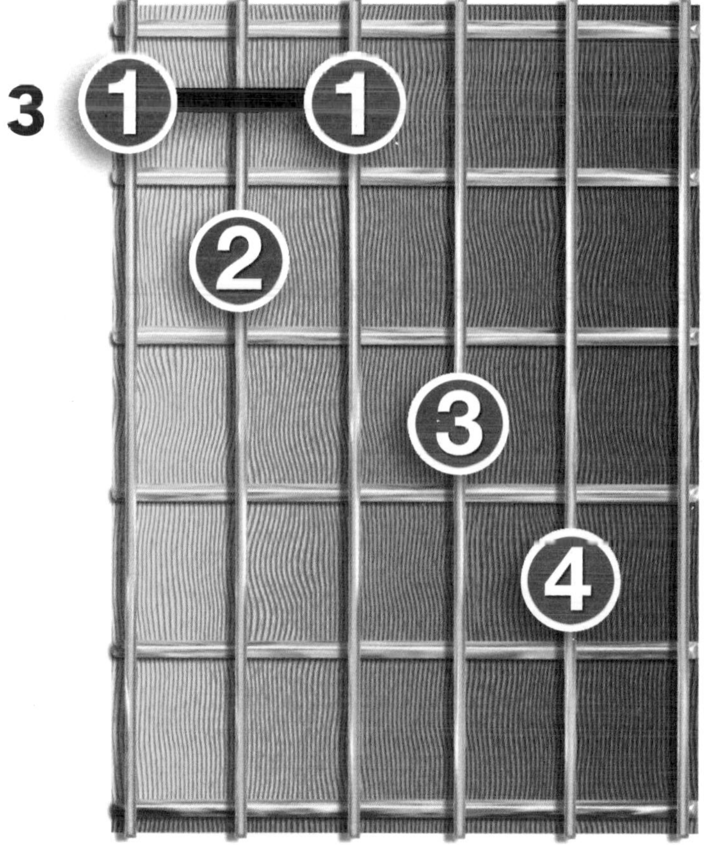


Bass String

### Chord Spelling

1st (E♭), 3rd (G), 5th (B♭)

**FREE ACCESS** on smartphones including iPhone & Android

Using any free QR code app, scan and **HEAR** the chord

# D♯/E♭m

## Minor

### Chord Spelling

1st (E♭), ♭3rd (G♭), 5th (B♭)

**FREE ACCESS** on smartphones including iPhone & Android

Using any free QR code app, scan and **HEAR** the chord

# D♯/E♭+
## Augmented Triad

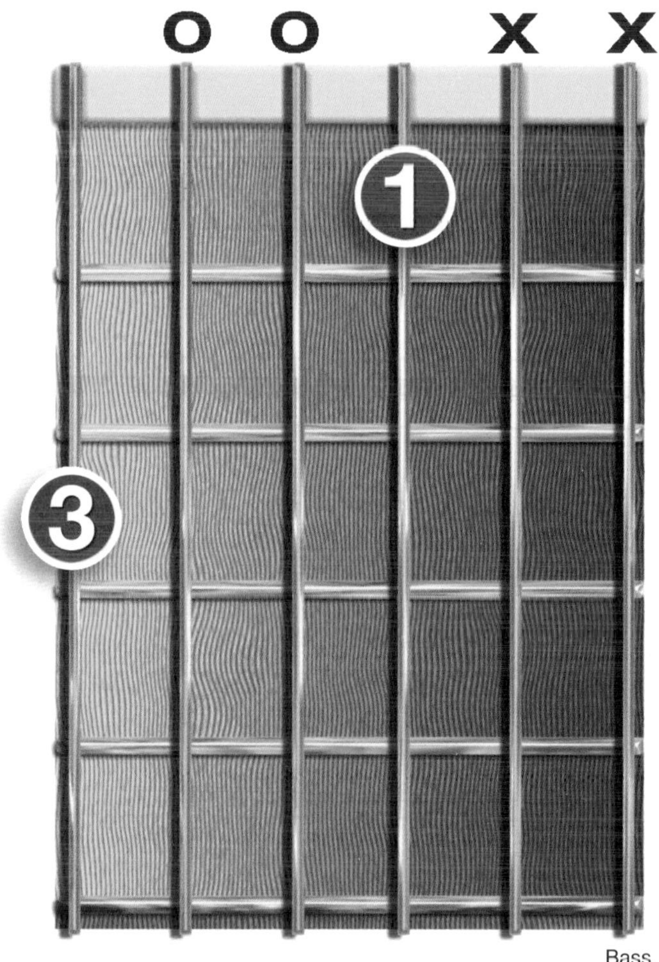


**Chord Spelling**

1st (E♭), 3rd (G), ♯5th (B)

**FREE ACCESS** on smartphones including iPhone & Android

Using any free QR code app, scan and **HEAR** the chord

# D♯/E♭°
## Diminished Triad

### Chord Spelling

1st (E♭), ♭3rd (G♭), ♭5th (B♭♭)

**FREE ACCESS** on smartphones including iPhone & Android

Using any free QR code app, scan and **HEAR** the chord

A
A♯/B♭
B
C
C♯/D♭
D
D♯/E♭
E
F
F♯/G♭
G
G♯/A♭

# D♯/E♭sus2

## Suspended 2nd

**Chord Spelling**

1st (E♭), 2nd (F), 5th (B♭)

**FREE ACCESS** on smartphones including iPhone & Android

Using any free QR code app, scan and **HEAR** the chord

# D♯/E♭sus4

## Suspended 4th

X X

3

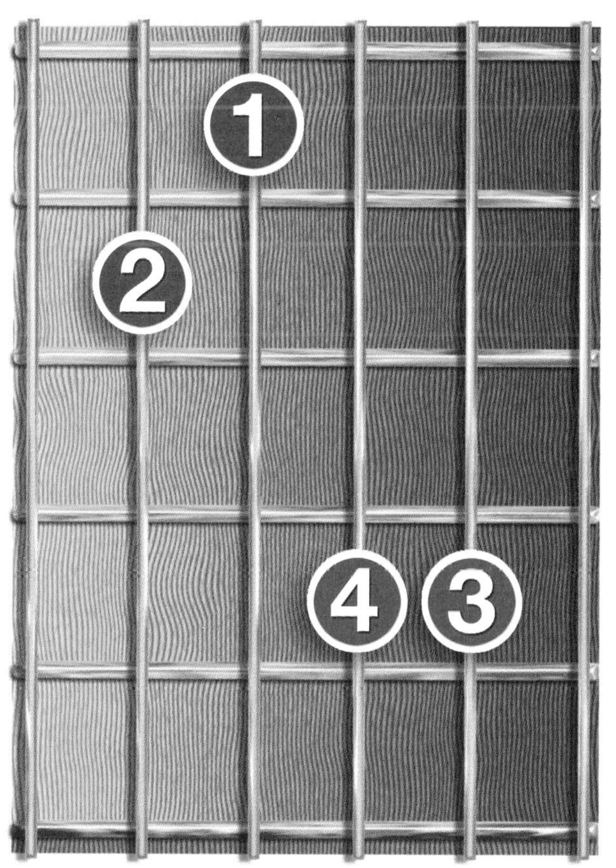


Bass String

**Chord Spelling**

1st (E♭), 4th (A♭), 5th (B♭)



**FREE ACCESS** on smartphones including iPhone & Android

Using any free QR code app, scan and **HEAR** the chord

# D♯/E♭5

## 5th (Power Chord)

X X 

6

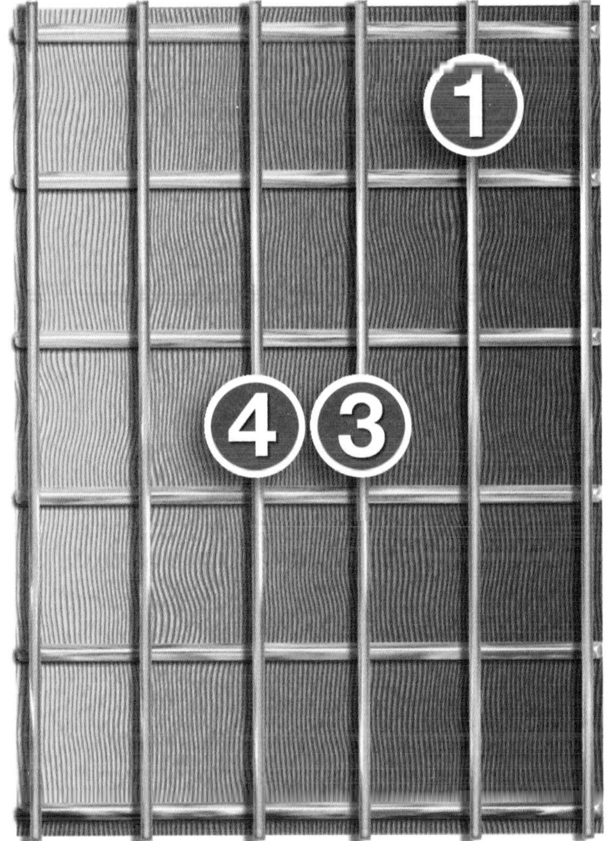


### Chord Spelling

1st (E♭), 5th (B♭)

**FREE ACCESS** on smartphones including iPhone & Android

Using any free QR code app, scan and **HEAR** the chord

# D♯/E♭6
## Major 6th

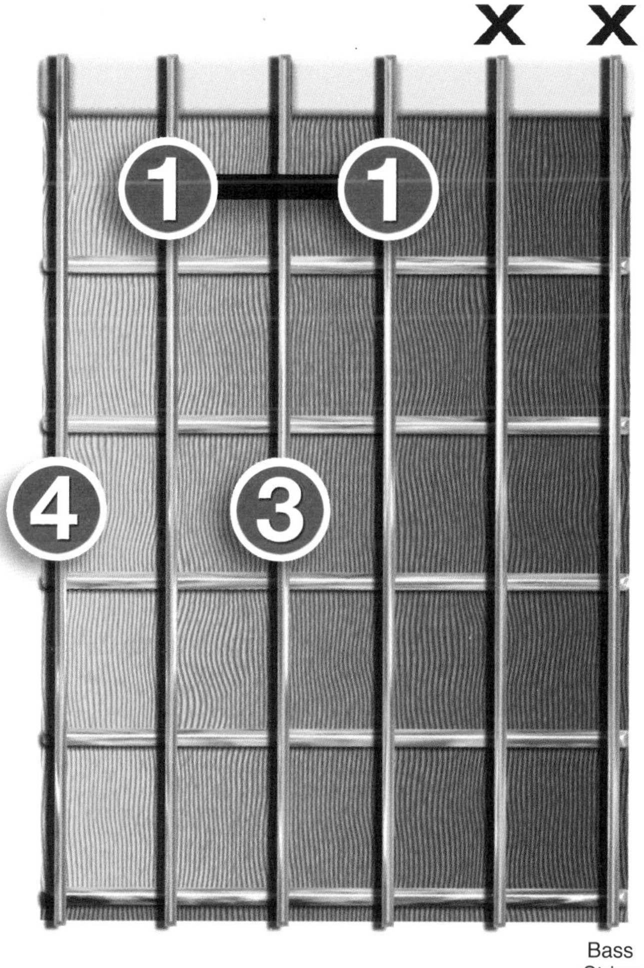


**Chord Spelling**

1st (E♭), 3rd (G), 5th (B♭), 6th (C)

**FREE ACCESS** on smartphones including iPhone & Android

Using any free QR code app, scan and **HEAR** the chord

# D♯/E♭m6

## Minor 6th

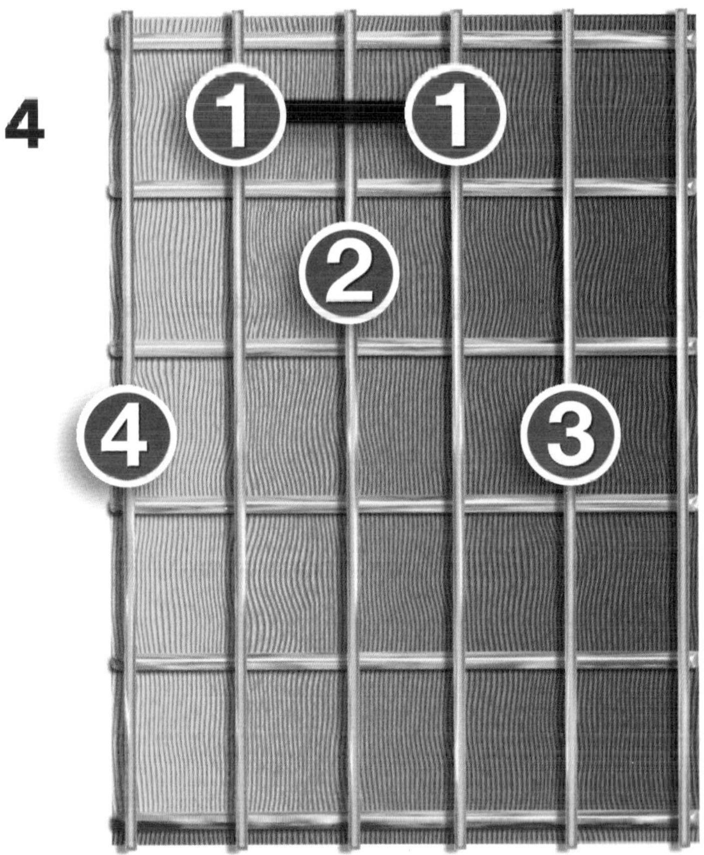


**Chord Spelling**

1st (E♭), ♭3rd (G♭), 5th (B♭), 6th (C)

**FREE ACCESS** on smartphones including iPhone & Android

Using any free QR code app, scan and **HEAR** the chord

# D♯/E♭maj7
## Major 7th

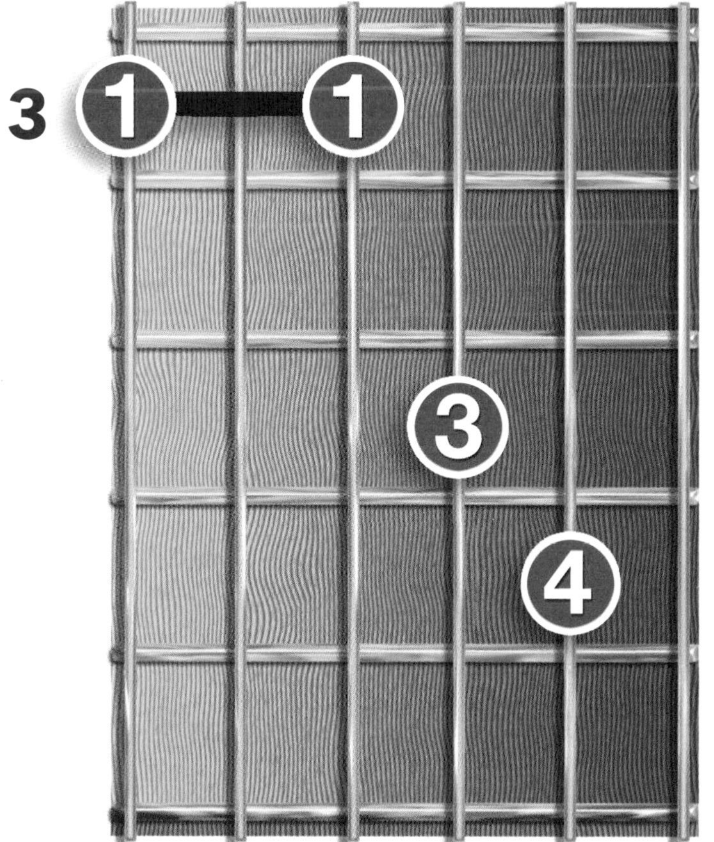


**Chord Spelling**

1st (E♭), 3rd (G), 5th (B♭), 7th (D)

**FREE ACCESS** on smartphones including iPhone & Android

Using any free QR code app, scan and **HEAR** the chord

D♯/E♭

# D♯/E♭m7

## Minor 7th

4

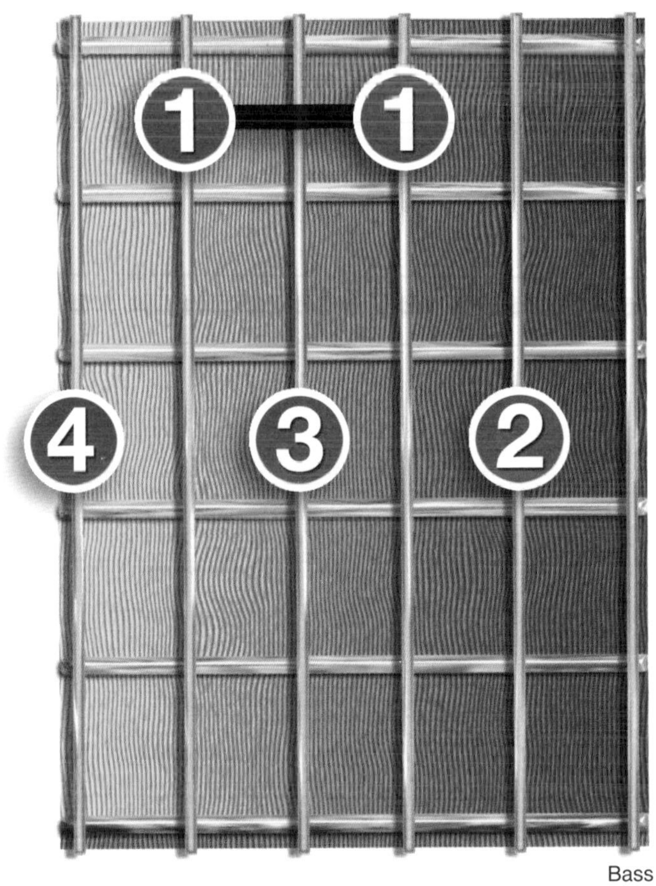


Bass String

**Chord Spelling**

1st (E♭), ♭3rd (G♭), 5th (B♭), ♭7th (D♭)

**FREE ACCESS** on smartphones including iPhone & Android

Using any free QR code app, scan and **HEAR** the chord

# D♯/E♭7
## Dominant 7th

4

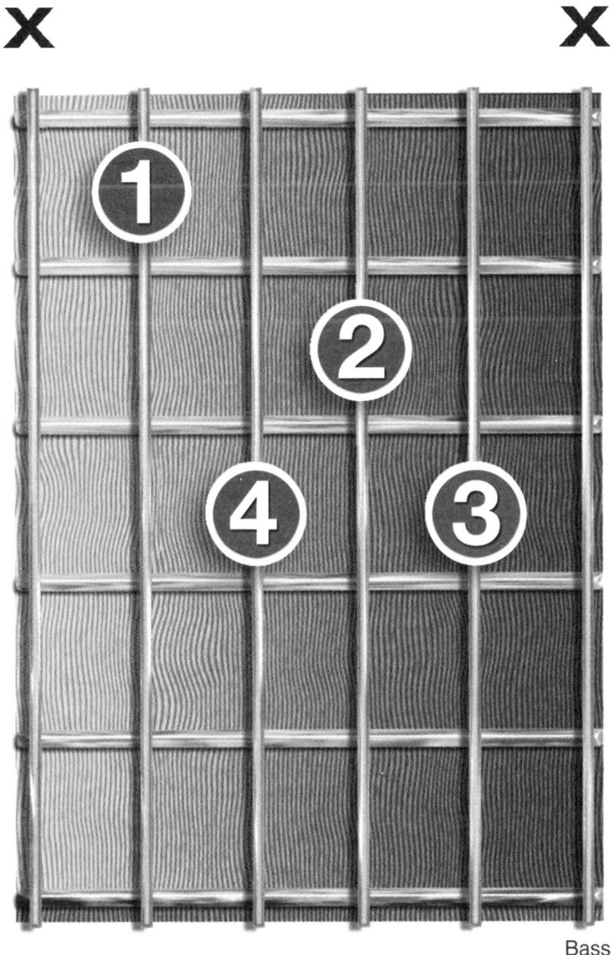


**Chord Spelling**

1st (E♭), 3rd (G), 5th (B♭), ♭7th (D♭)

**FREE ACCESS** on smartphones including iPhone & Android

Using any free QR code app, scan and **HEAR** the chord

# D♯/E♭°7
## Diminished 7th

### Chord Spelling

1st (E♭), ♭3rd (G♭), ♭5th (B♭♭), ♭♭7th (D♭♭)

**FREE ACCESS** on smartphones including iPhone & Android

Using any free QR code app, scan and **HEAR** the chord

# D♯/E♭maj9

## Major 9th

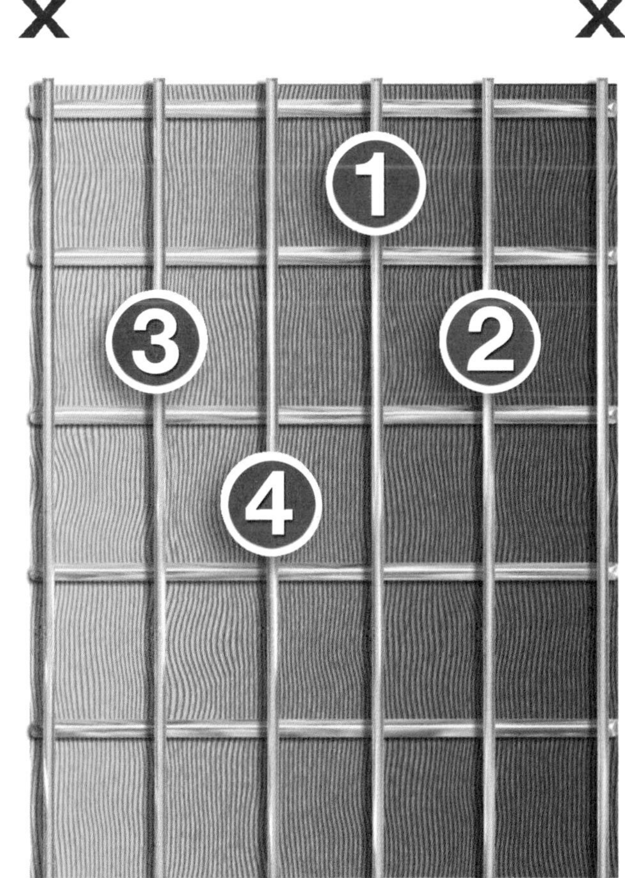


### Chord Spelling

1st (E♭), 3rd (G), 5th (B♭), 7th (D), 9th (F)

**FREE ACCESS** on smartphones including iPhone & Android

Using any free QR code app, scan and **HEAR** the chord

D♯/E♭

A
A♯/B♭
B
C
C♯/D♭
D
D♯/E♭
E
F
F♯/G♭
G
G♯/A♭

# E
## Major

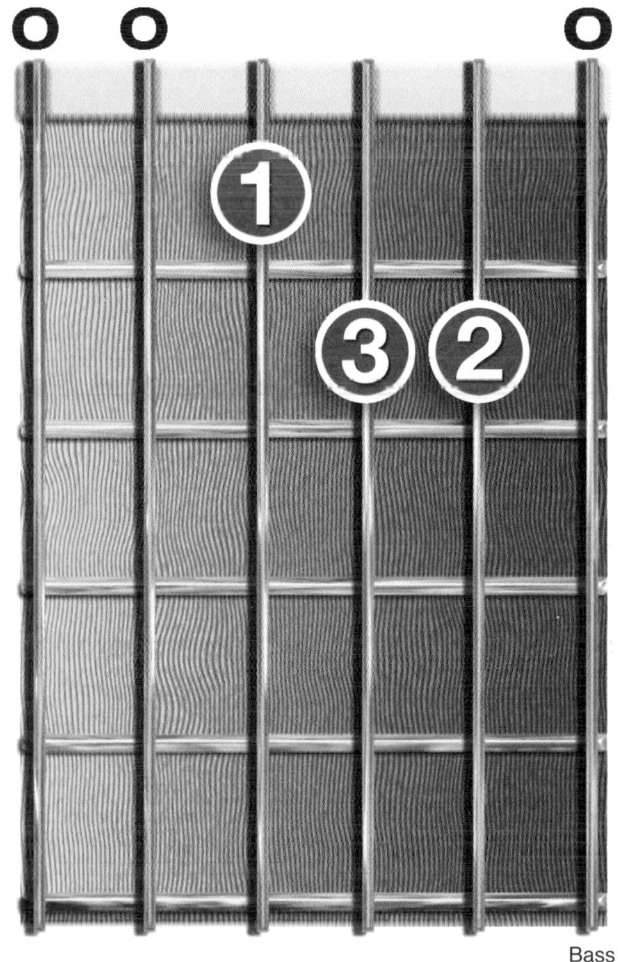


**Chord Spelling**

1st (E), 3rd (G♯), 5th (B)

**FREE ACCESS** on smartphones including iPhone & Android

Using any free QR code app, scan and **HEAR** the chord

# Em

## Minor

### Chord Spelling

1st (E), ♭3rd (G), 5th (B)

**FREE ACCESS** on smartphones including iPhone & Android

Using any free QR code app, scan and **HEAR** the chord

# E+

## Augmented Triad

o o

5

1 1 2 3

Bass String

**Chord Spelling**

1st (E), 3rd (G♯), ♯5th (B♯)

**FREE ACCESS** on smartphones including iPhone & Android

Using any free QR code app, scan and **HEAR** the chord

# E°

## Diminished Triad

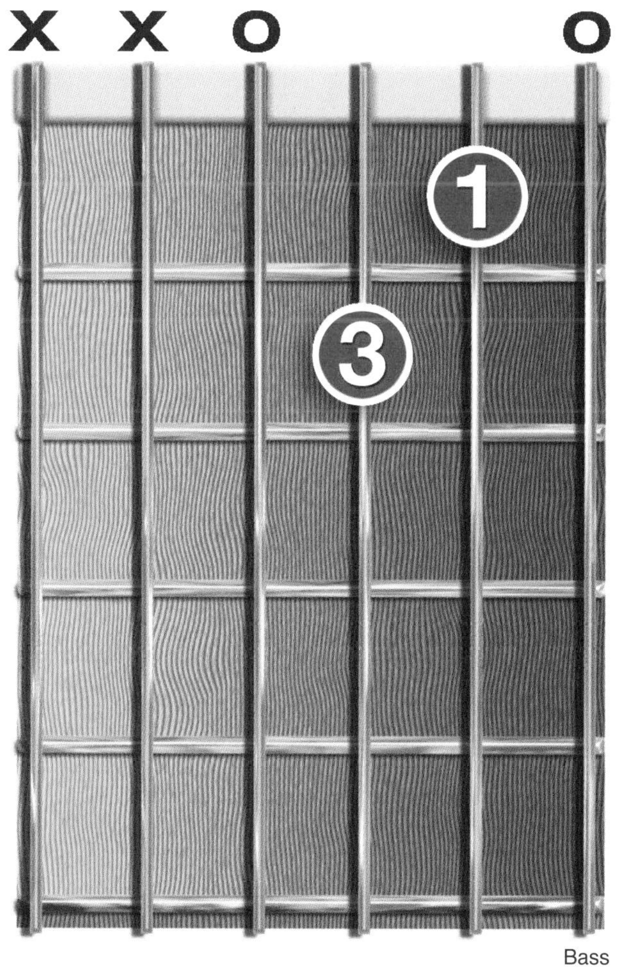


### Chord Spelling

1st (E), ♭3rd (G), ♭5th (B♭)

**FREE ACCESS** on smartphones including iPhone & Android

Using any free QR code app, scan and **HEAR** the chord

A
A♯/B♭
B
C
C♯/D♭
D
D♯/E♭
E
F
F♯/G♭
G
G♯/A♭

# Esus2

## Suspended 2nd

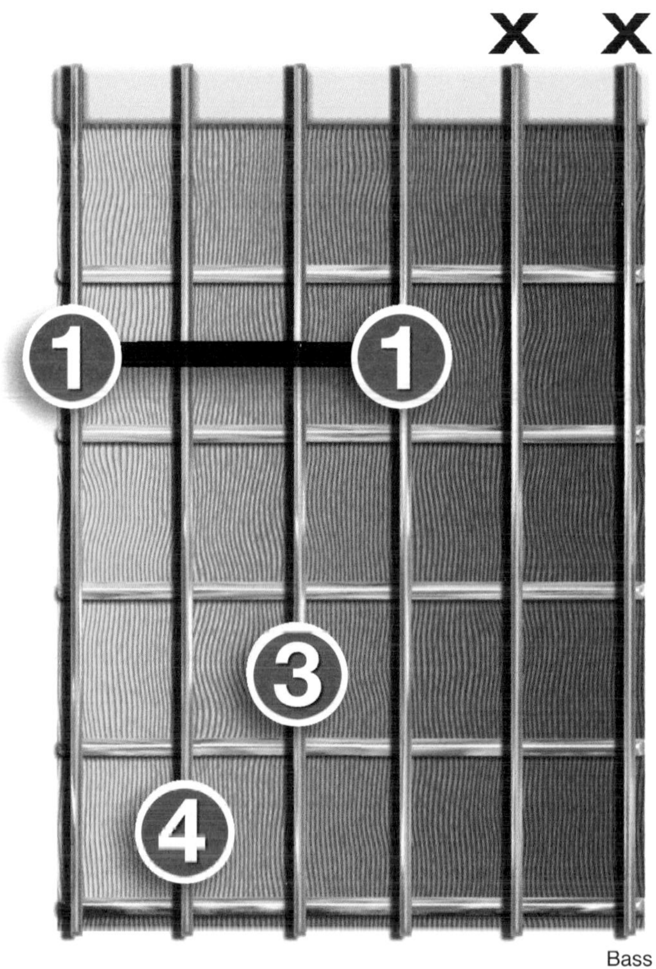


**Chord Spelling**

1st (E), 2nd (F♯), 5th (B)

**FREE ACCESS** on smartphones including iPhone & Android

Using any free QR code app, scan and **HEAR** the chord

# Esus4

## Suspended 4th

**Chord Spelling**

1st (E), 4th (A), 5th (B)

**FREE ACCESS** on smartphones including iPhone & Android

Using any free QR code app, scan and **HEAR** the chord

# E5

## 5th (Power Chord)

**Chord Spelling**

1st (E), 5th (B)

**FREE ACCESS** on smartphones including iPhone & Android

Using any free QR code app, scan and **HEAR** the chord

# E6

## Major 6th

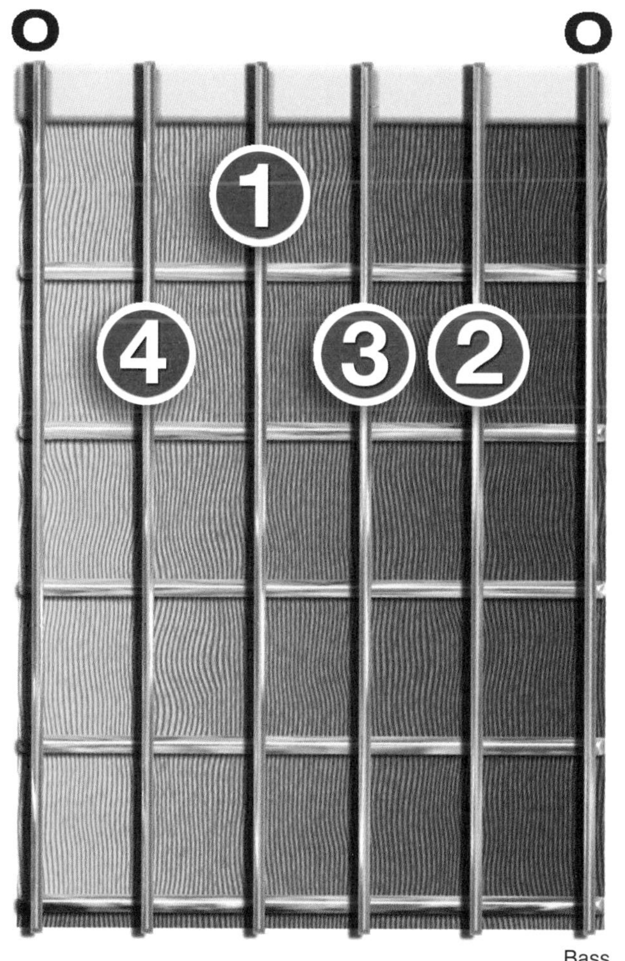


**Chord Spelling**

1st (E), 3rd (G♯), 5th (B), 6th (C♯)

**FREE ACCESS** on smartphones including iPhone & Android

Using any free QR code app, scan and **HEAR** the chord

# Em6

## Minor 6th

**Chord Spelling**

1st (E), ♭3rd (G), 5th (B), 6th (C♯)

**FREE ACCESS** on smartphones including iPhone & Android

Using any free QR code app, scan and **HEAR** the chord

# Emaj7

## Major 7th

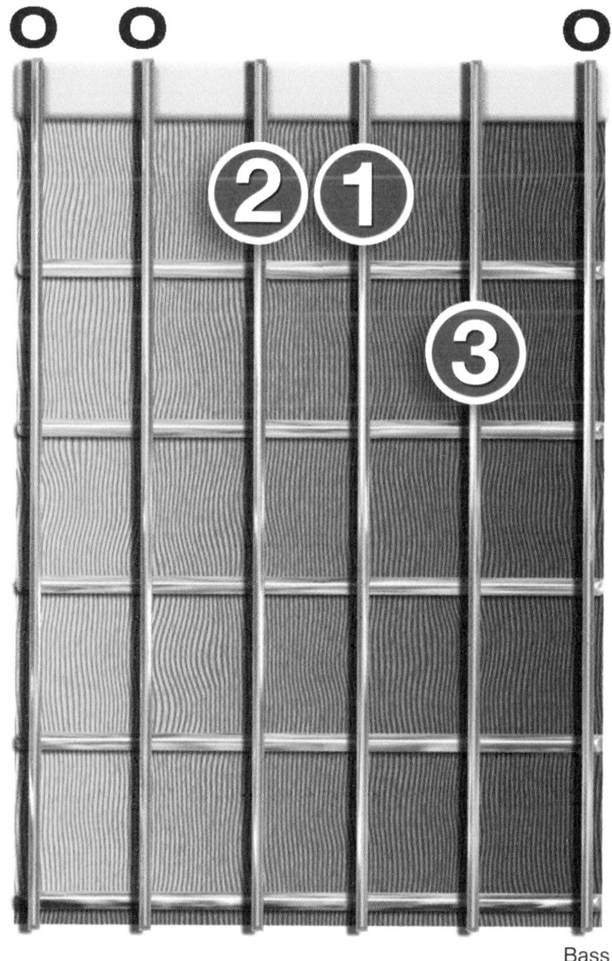


### Chord Spelling

1st (E), 3rd (G♯), 5th (B), 7th (D♯)

**FREE ACCESS** on smartphones including iPhone & Android

Using any free QR code app, scan and **HEAR** the chord

# Em7

## Minor 7th

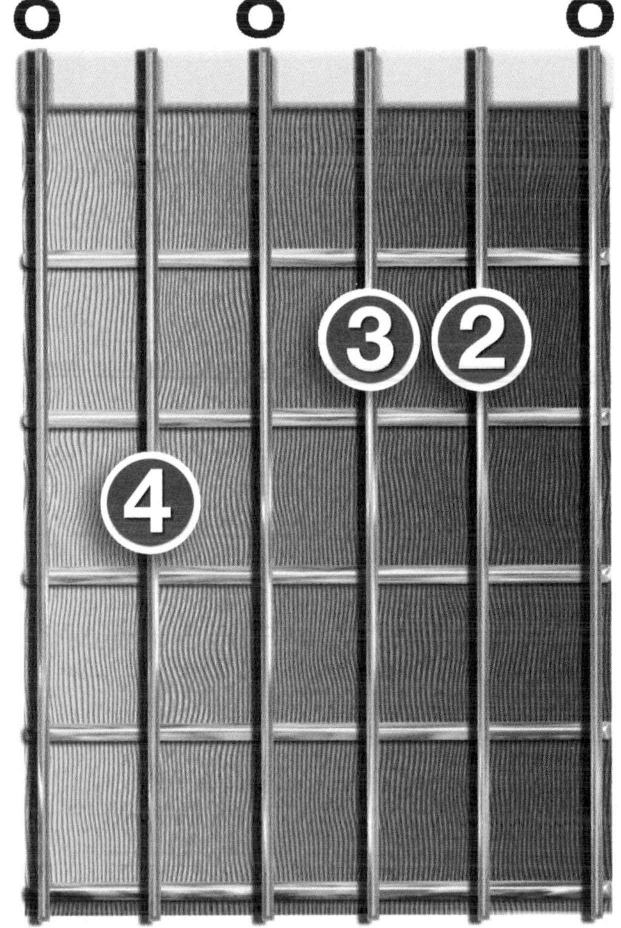


**Chord Spelling**

1st (E), ♭3rd (G), 5th (B), ♭7th (D)

**FREE ACCESS** on smartphones including iPhone & Android

Using any free QR code app, scan and **HEAR** the chord

# E7

## Dominant 7th

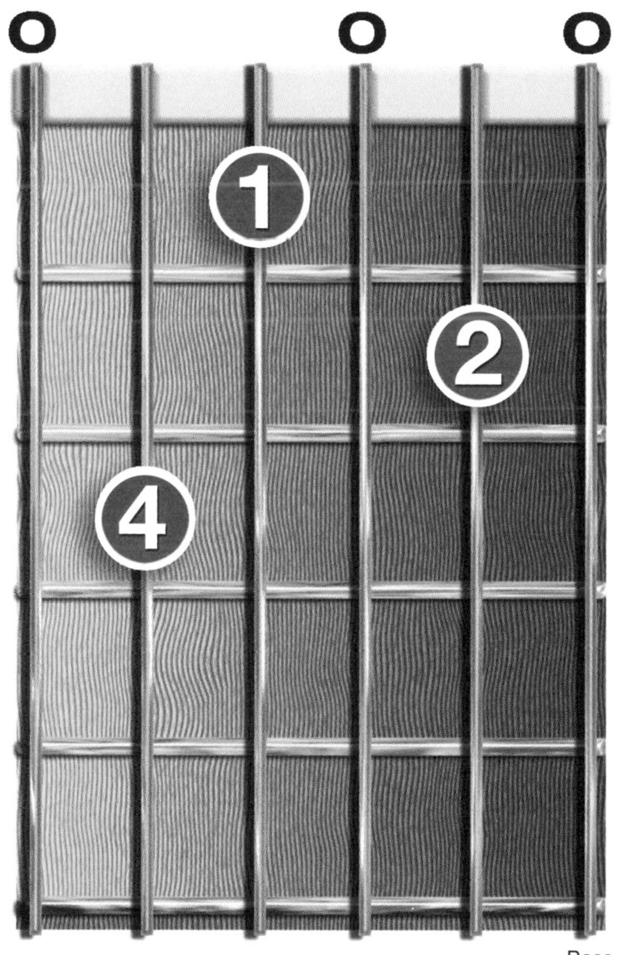


**Chord Spelling**

1st (E), 3rd (G♯), 5th (B), ♭7th (D)

**FREE ACCESS** on smartphones including iPhone & Android

Using any free QR code app, scan and **HEAR** the chord

# E°7

## Diminished 7th

**Chord Spelling**

1st (E), ♭3rd (G), ♭5th (B♭), 𝄫7th (D♭)

**FREE ACCESS** on smartphones including iPhone & Android

Using any free QR code app, scan and **HEAR** the chord

# Emaj9

## Major 9th

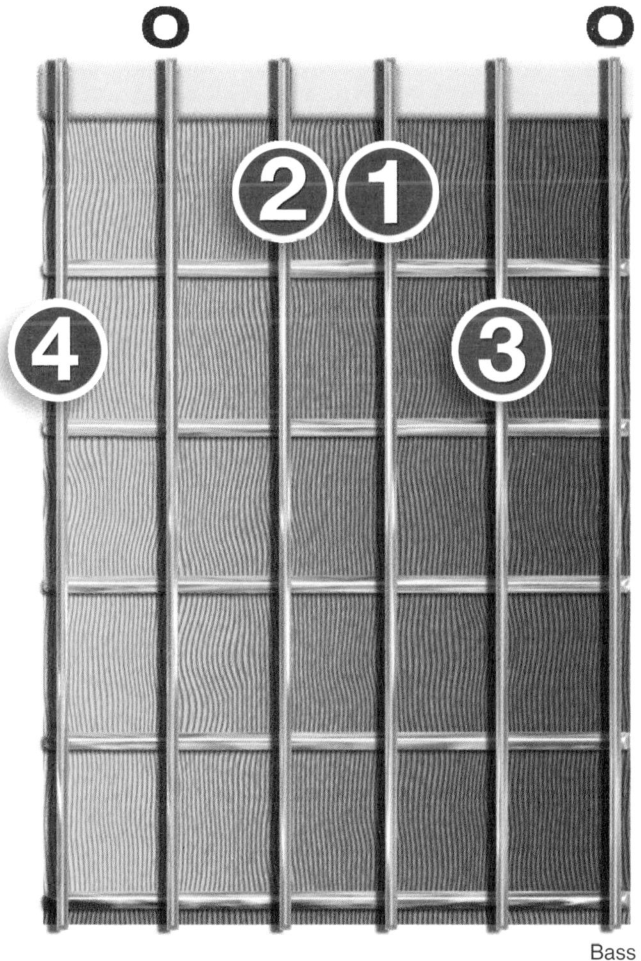


**Chord Spelling**

1st (E), 3rd (G♯), 5th (B), 7th (D♯), 9th (F♯)

**FREE ACCESS** on smartphones including iPhone & Android

Using any free QR code app, scan and **HEAR** the chord

E

A
A♯/B♭
B
C
C♯/D♭
D
D♯/E♭
E
F
F♯/G♭
G
G♯/A♭

# F

## Major

**Chord Spelling**

1st (F), 3rd (A), 5th (C)

**FREE ACCESS** on smartphones including iPhone & Android

Using any free QR code app, scan and **HEAR** the chord

# Fm

## Minor

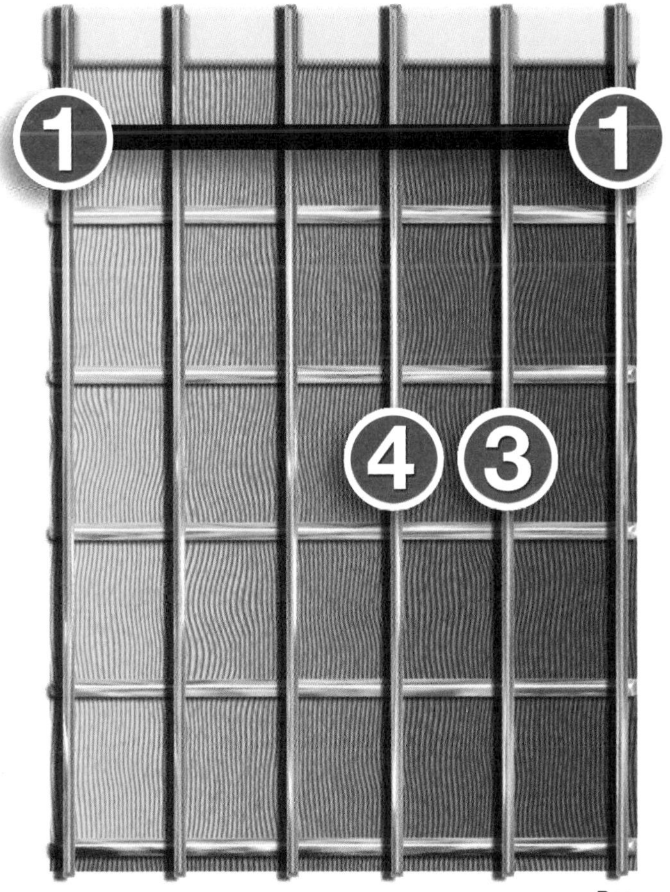


**Chord Spelling**

1st (F), ♭3rd (A♭), 5th (C)

**FREE ACCESS** on smartphones including iPhone & Android

Using any free QR code app, scan and **HEAR** the chord

# F+

## Augmented Triad

**Chord Spelling**

1st (F), 3rd (A), ♯5th (C♯)

**FREE ACCESS** on smartphones including iPhone & Android

Using any free QR code app, scan and **HEAR** the chord

# F°

## Diminished Triad

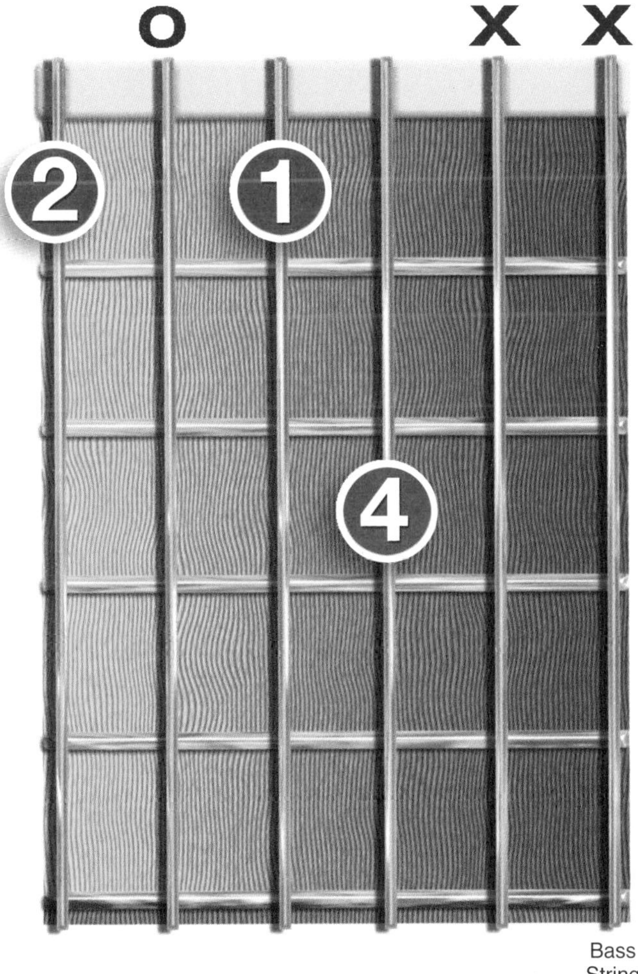


**Chord Spelling**

1st (F), ♭3rd (A♭), ♭5th (C♭)

**FREE ACCESS** on smartphones including iPhone & Android

Using any free QR code app, scan and **HEAR** the chord

F

A
A♯/B♭
B
C
C♯/D♭
D
D♯/E♭
E
F
F♯/G♭
G
G♯/A♭

# Fsus2

## Suspended 2nd

**Chord Spelling**

1st (F), 2nd (G), 5th (C)

**FREE ACCESS** on smartphones including iPhone & Android

Using any free QR code app, scan and **HEAR** the chord

# Fsus4

## Suspended 4th

**Chord Spelling**

1st (F), 4th (B♭), 5th (C)

**FREE ACCESS** on smartphones including iPhone & Android

Using any free QR code app, scan and **HEAR** the chord

# F5

## 5th (Power Chord)

**Chord Spelling**

1st (F), 5th (C)

**FREE ACCESS** on smartphones including iPhone & Android

Using any free QR code app, scan and **HEAR** the chord

# F6

## Major 6th

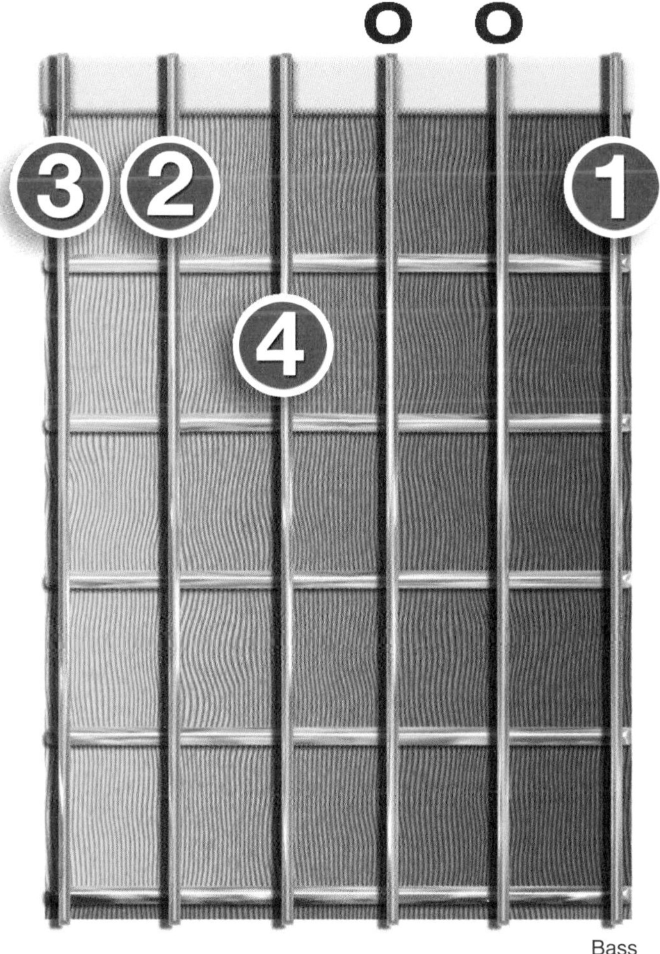


**Chord Spelling**

1st (F), 3rd (A), 5th (C), 6th (D)

**FREE ACCESS** on smartphones including iPhone & Android

Using any free QR code app, scan and **HEAR** the chord

A

A♯/B♭

B

C

C♯/D♭

D

D♯/E♭

E

F

F♯/G♭

G

G♯/A♭

# Fm6

## Minor 6th

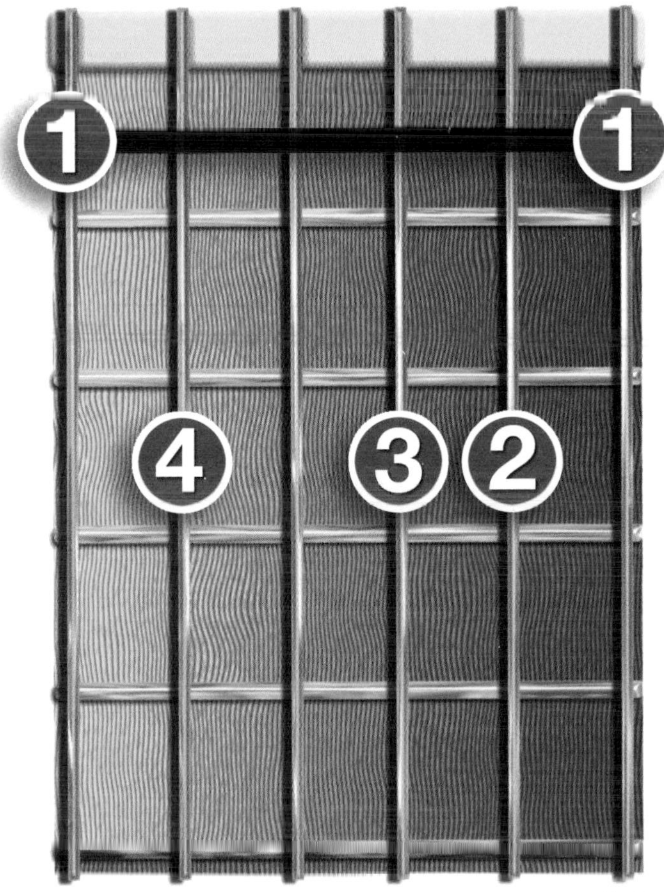


**Chord Spelling**

1st (F), ♭3rd (A♭), 5th (C), 6th (D)

**FREE ACCESS** on smartphones including iPhone & Android

Using any free QR code app, scan and **HEAR** the chord

# Fmaj7

## Major 7th

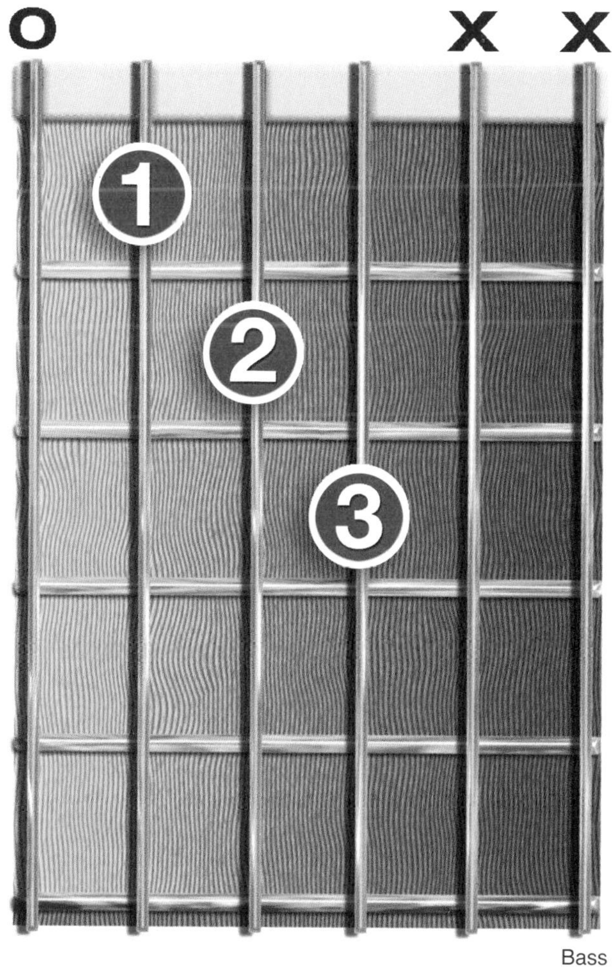


### Chord Spelling

1st (F), 3rd (A), 5th (C), 7th (E)

**FREE ACCESS** on smartphones including iPhone & Android

Using any free QR code app, scan and **HEAR** the chord

# Fm7

## Minor 7th

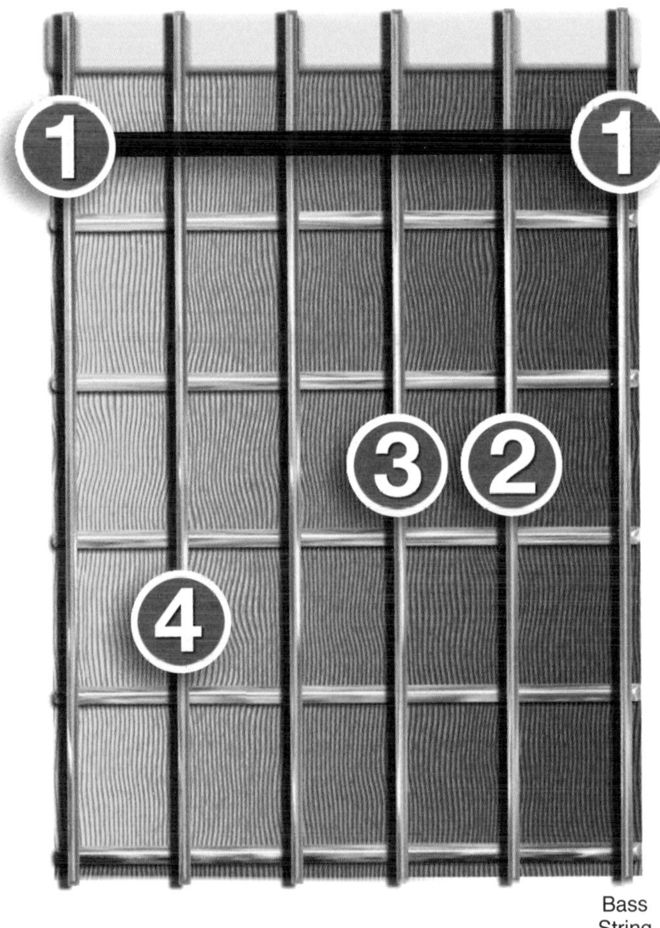


**Chord Spelling**

1st (F), ♭3rd (A♭), 5th (C), ♭7th (E♭)

**FREE ACCESS** on smartphones including iPhone & Android

Using any free QR code app, scan and **HEAR** the chord

# F7
## Dominant 7th

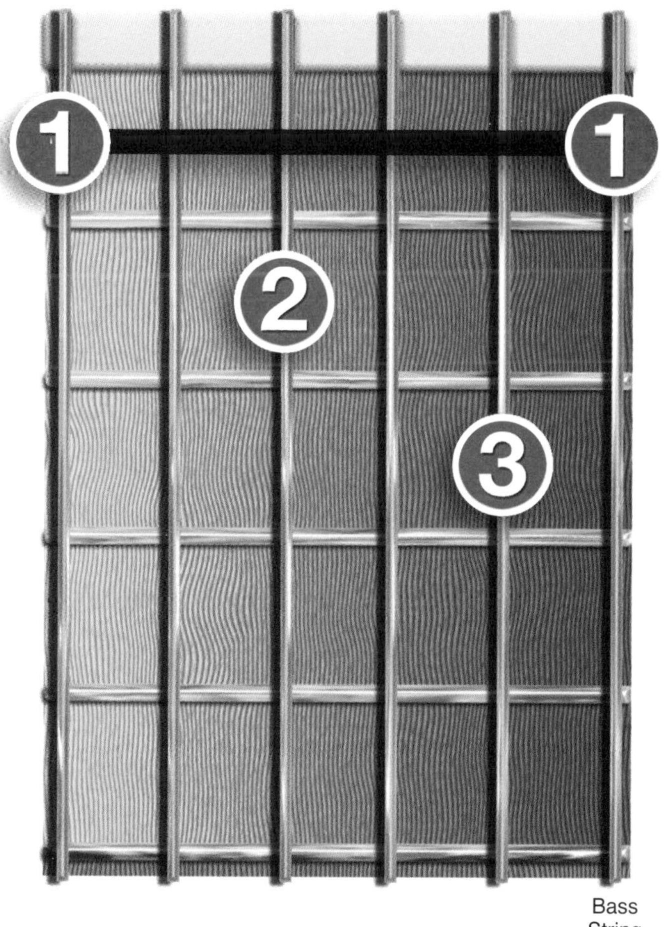


### Chord Spelling

1st (F), 3rd (A), 5th (C), ♭7th (E♭)

**FREE ACCESS** on smartphones including iPhone & Android

Using any free QR code app, scan and **HEAR** the chord

# F°7

## Diminished 7th

x x

3

2 1

4 3

Bass String

### Chord Spelling

1st (F), ♭3rd (A♭), ♭5th (C♭), ♭♭7th (E♭♭)

**FREE ACCESS** on smartphones including iPhone & Android

Using any free QR code app, scan and **HEAR** the chord

# Fmaj9
## Major 9th

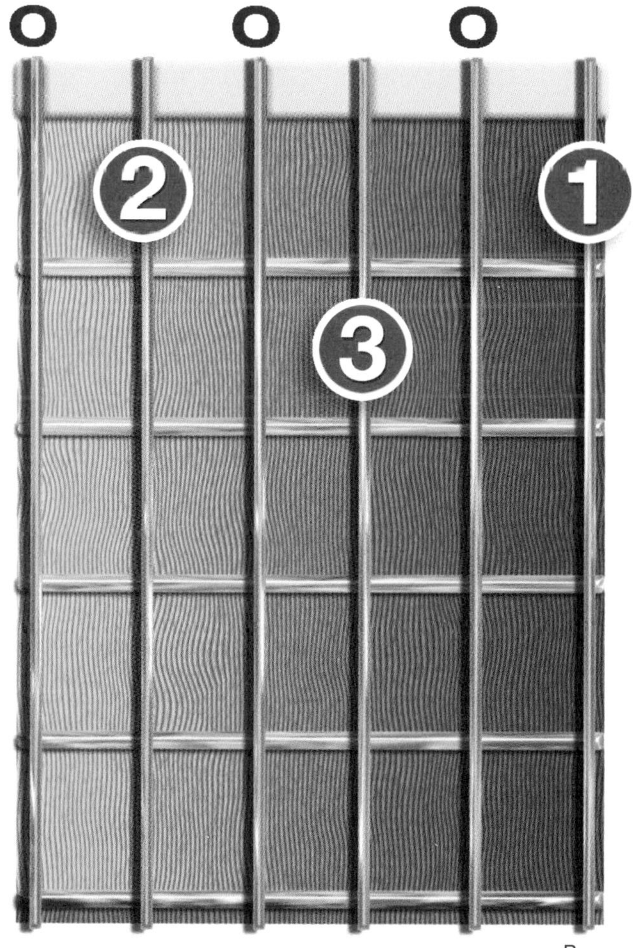


### Chord Spelling

1st (F), 3rd (A), 5th (C), 7th (E), 9th (G)

**FREE ACCESS** on smartphones including iPhone & Android

Using any free QR code app, scan and **HEAR** the chord

# F♯/G♭
## Major

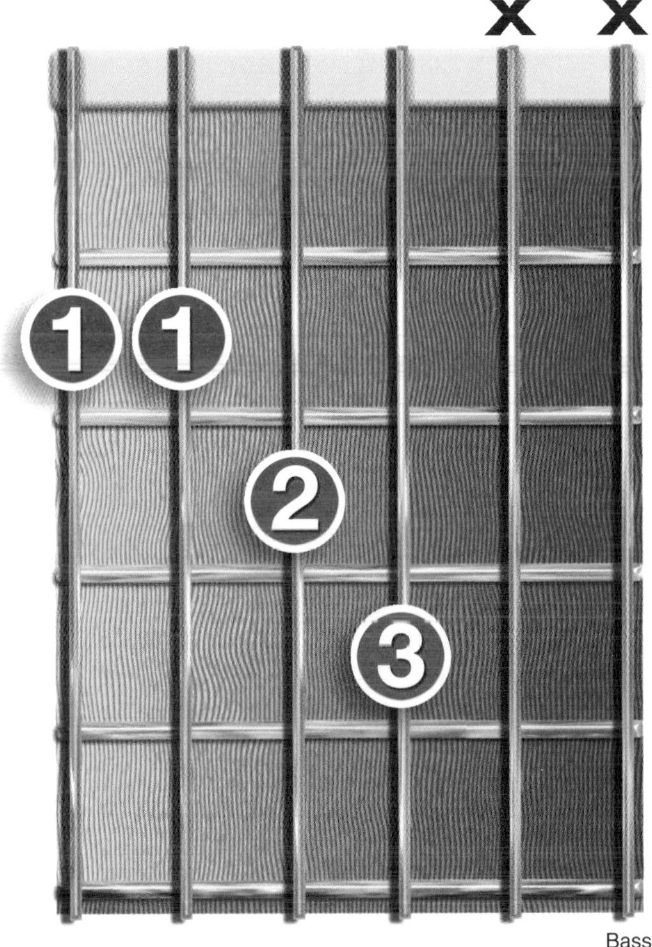


**Chord Spelling**

1st (F♯), 3rd (A♯), 5th (C♯)

**FREE ACCESS** on smartphones including iPhone & Android

Using any free QR code app, scan and **HEAR** the chord

# F♯/G♭m
## Minor

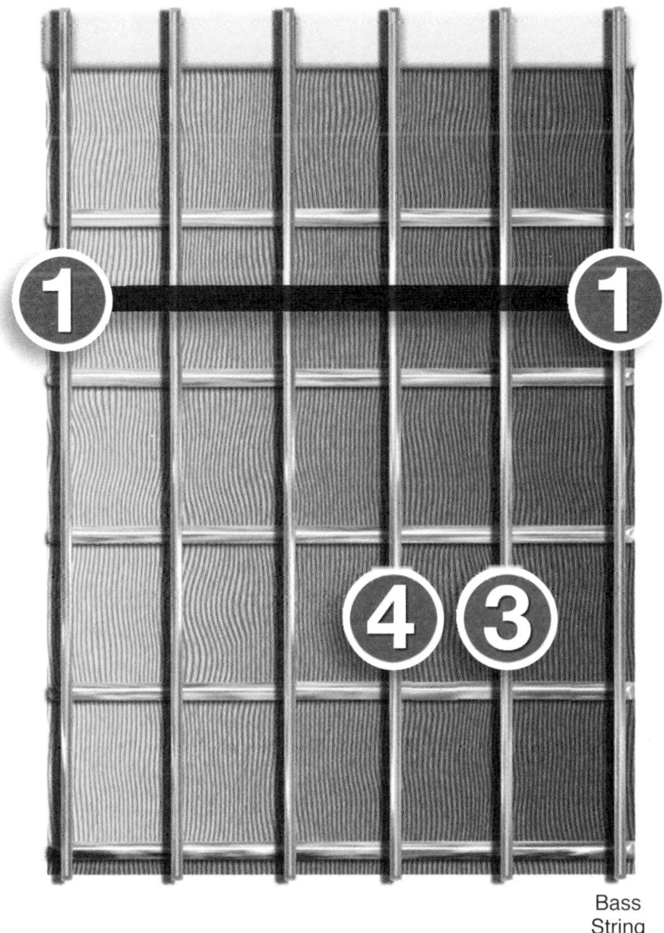


**Chord Spelling**

1st (F♯), ♭3rd (A), 5th (C♯)

**FREE ACCESS** on smartphones including iPhone & Android

Using any free QR code app, scan and **HEAR** the chord

# F♯/G♭+

## Augmented Triad

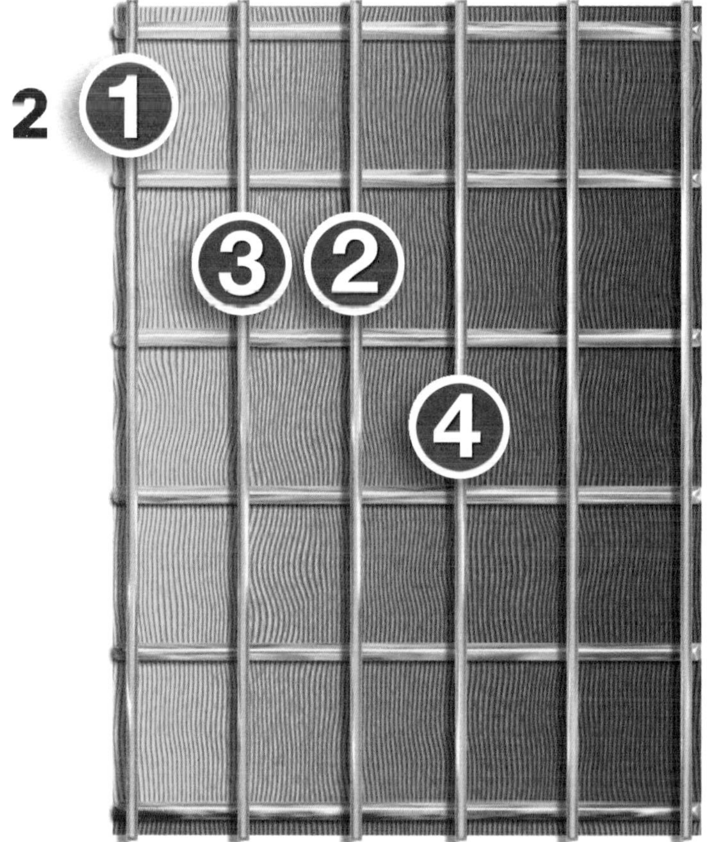


**Chord Spelling**

1st (F♯), 3rd (A♯), ♯5th (C𝄪)

**FREE ACCESS** on smartphones including iPhone & Android

Using any free QR code app, scan and **HEAR** the chord

# F♯/G♭°

## Diminished Triad

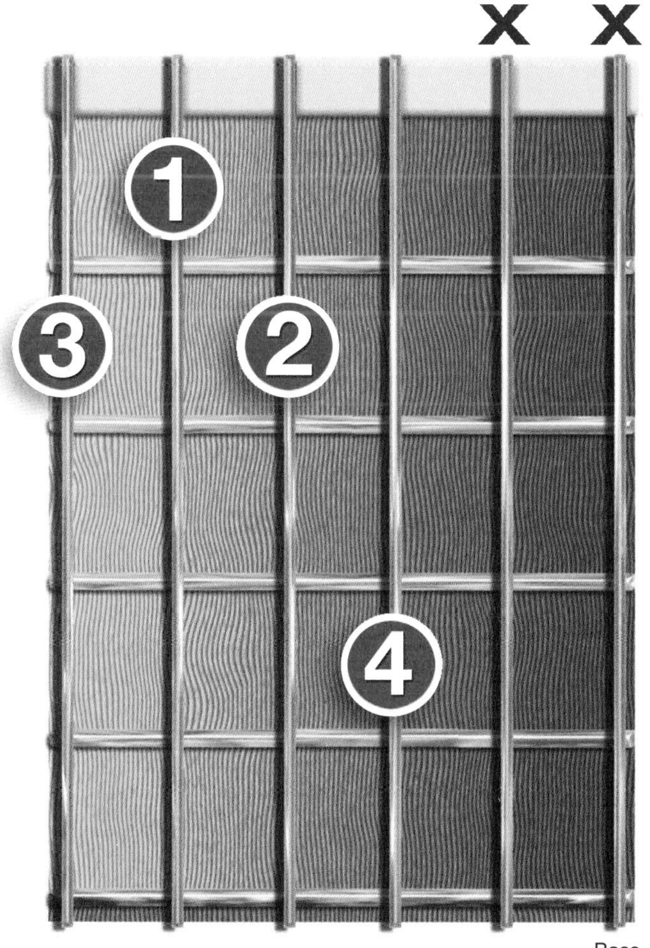


### Chord Spelling

1st (F♯), ♭3rd (A), ♭5th (C)

**FREE ACCESS** on smartphones including iPhone & Android

Using any free QR code app, scan and **HEAR** the chord

# F♯/G♭sus2

## Suspended 2nd

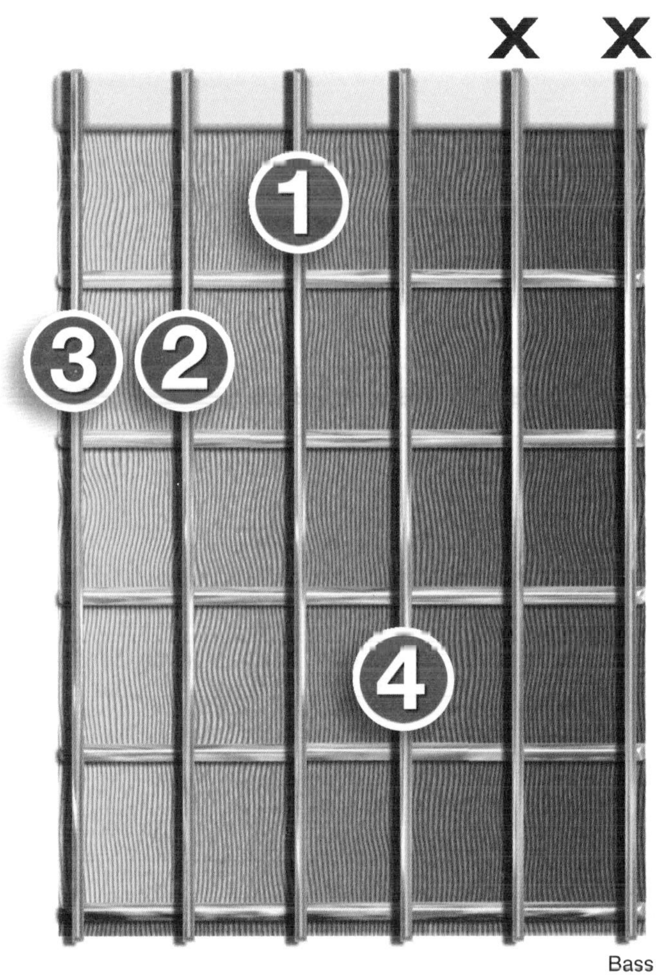


### Chord Spelling

1st (F♯), 2nd (G♯), 5th (C♯)

**FREE ACCESS** on smartphones including iPhone & Android

Using any free QR code app, scan and **HEAR** the chord

# F♯/G♭sus4

## Suspended 4th

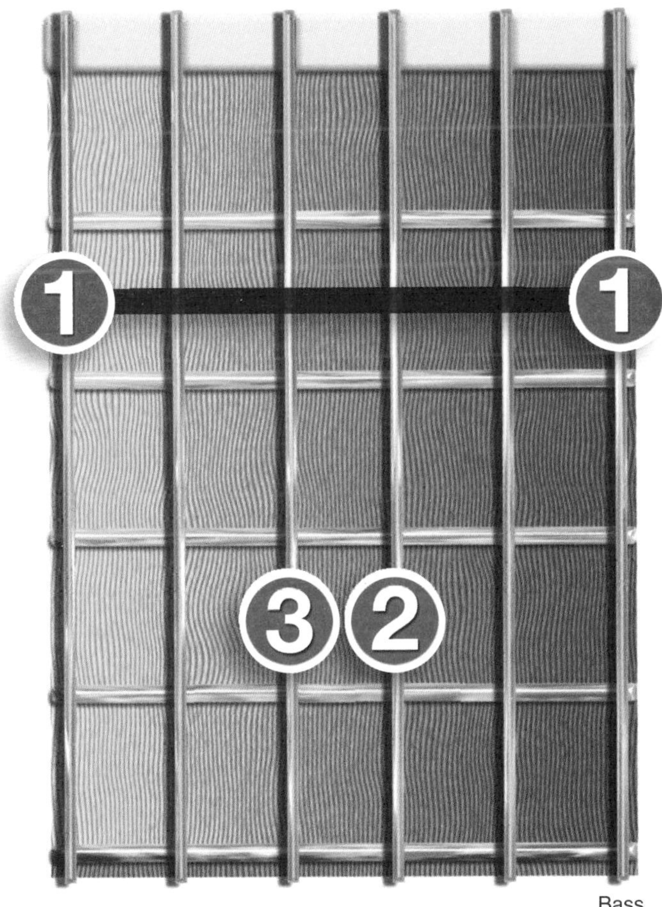


**Chord Spelling**

1st (F♯), 4th (B), 5th (C♯)

**FREE ACCESS** on smartphones including iPhone & Android

Using any free QR code app, scan and **HEAR** the chord

# F♯/G♭5

## 5th (Power Chord)

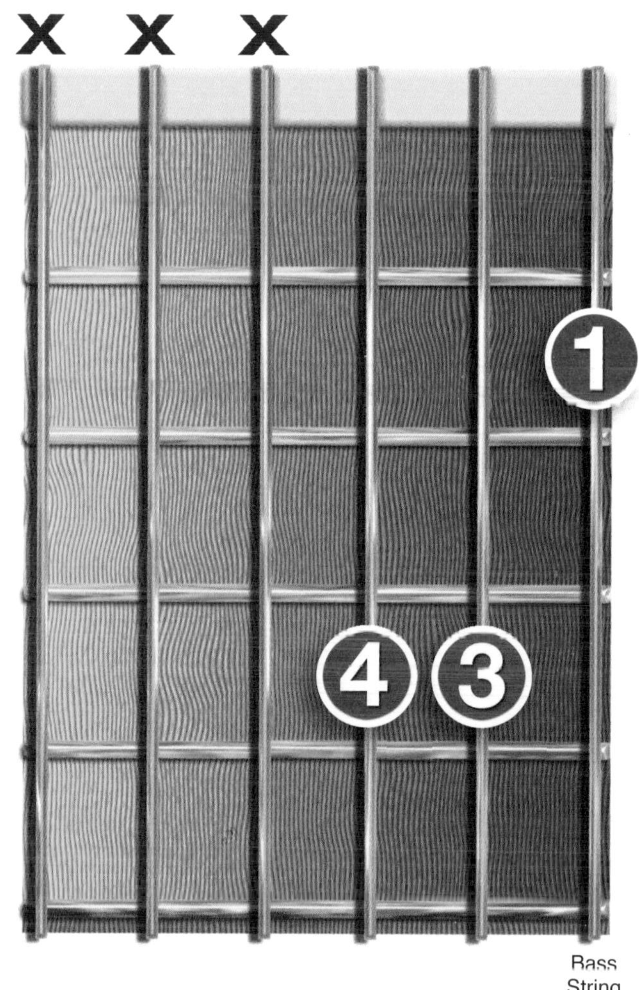


**Chord Spelling**

1st (F♯), 5th (C♯)

**FREE ACCESS** on smartphones including iPhone & Android

Using any free QR code app, scan and **HEAR** the chord

# F♯/G♭6
## Major 6th

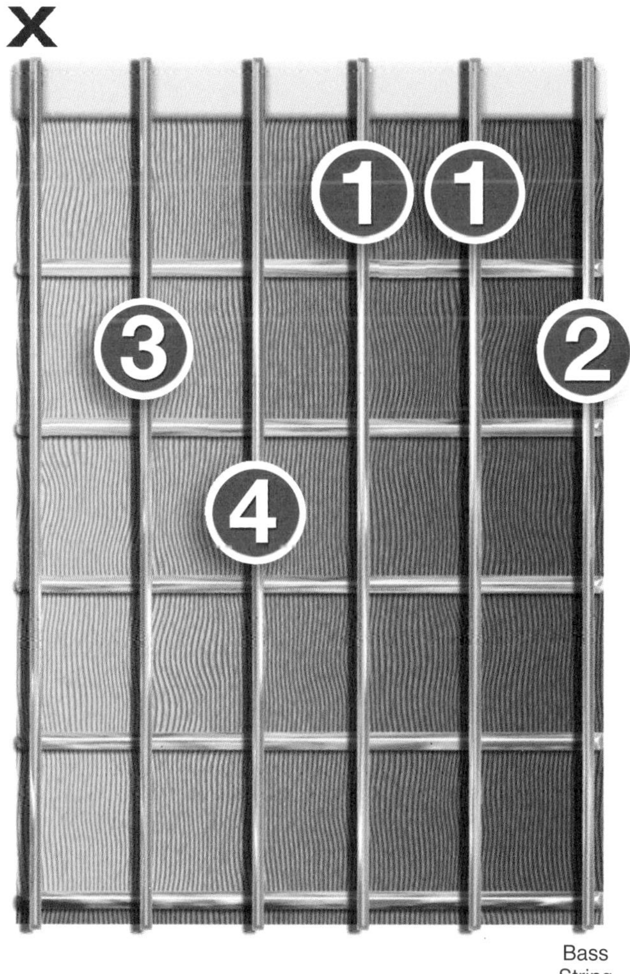


**Chord Spelling**

1st (F♯), 3rd (A♯), 5th (C♯), 6th (D♯)

**FREE ACCESS** on smartphones including iPhone & Android

Using any free QR code app, scan and **HEAR** the chord

# F♯/G♭m6

## Minor 6th

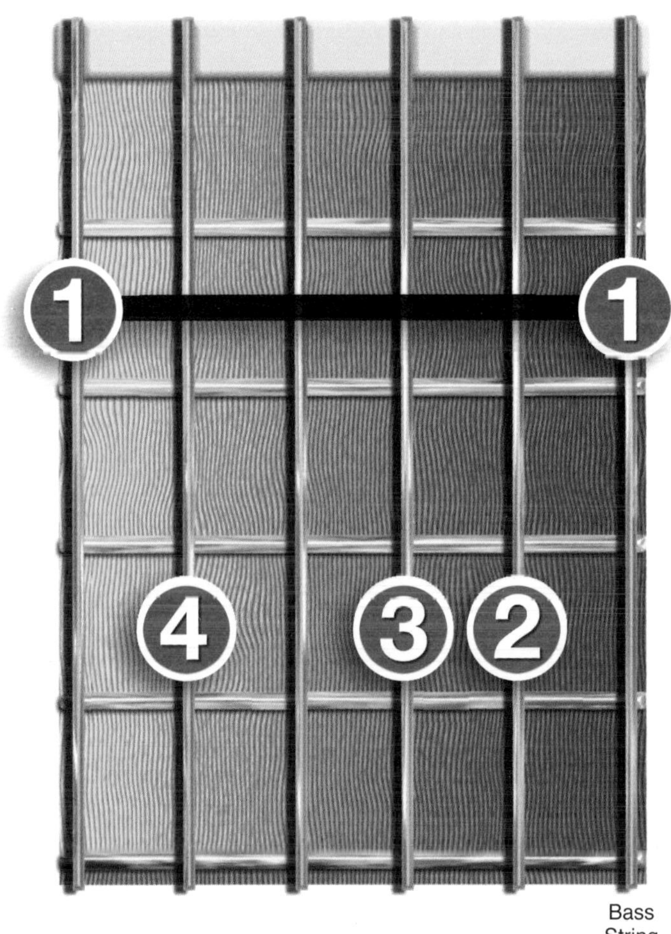


**Chord Spelling**

1st (F♯), ♭3rd (A), 5th (C♯), 6th (D♯)

**FREE ACCESS** on smartphones including iPhone & Android

Using any free QR code app, scan and **HEAR** the chord

# F♯/G♭maj7

## Major 7th

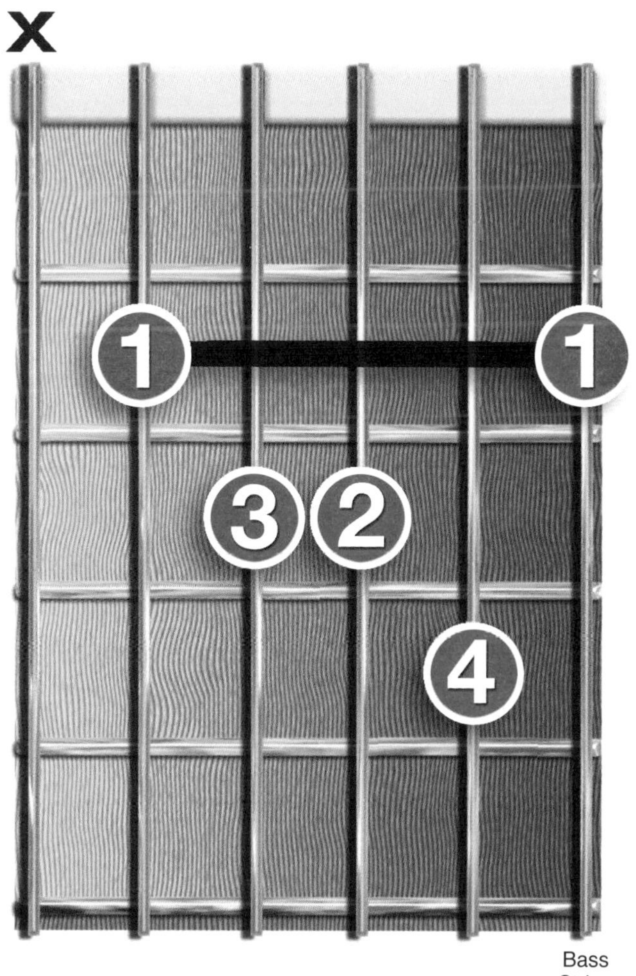


**Chord Spelling**

1st (F♯), 3rd (A♯), 5th (C♯), 7th (F)

**FREE ACCESS** on smartphones including iPhone & Android

Using any free QR code app, scan and **HEAR** the chord

# F♯/G♭m7

## Minor 7th

### Chord Spelling

1st (F♯), ♭3rd (A), 5th (C♯), ♭7th (E)

**FREE ACCESS** on smartphones including iPhone & Android

Using any free QR code app, scan and **HEAR** the chord

# F♯/G♭7

## Dominant 7th

**Chord Spelling**

1st (F♯), 3rd (A♯), 5th (C♯), ♭7th (E)

**FREE ACCESS** on smartphones including iPhone & Android

Using any free QR code app, scan and **HEAR** the chord

# F♯/G♭°7

## Diminished 7th

4

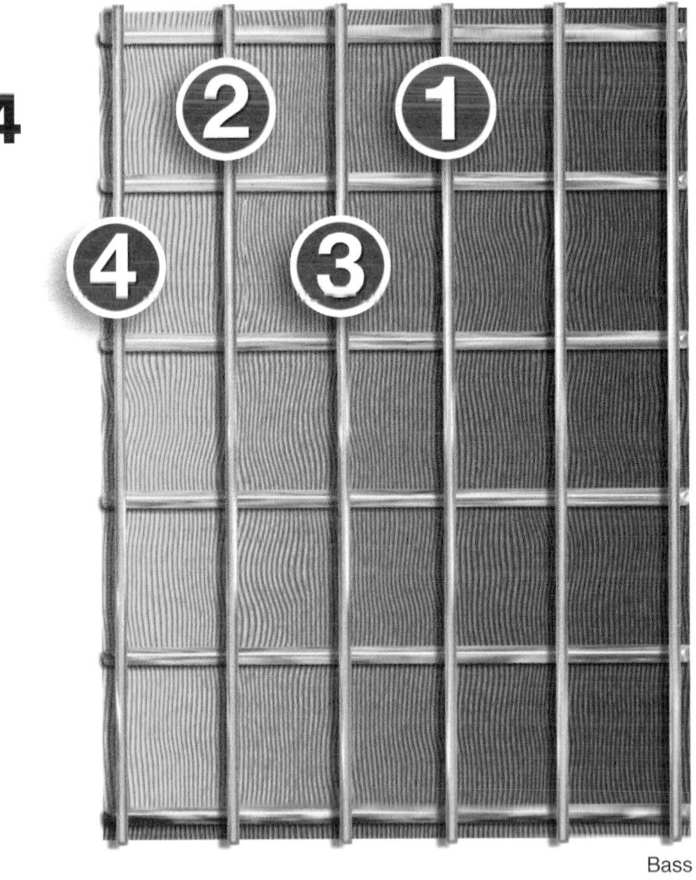

Bass String

**Chord Spelling**

1st (F♯), ♭3rd (A), ♭5th (C), 𝄫7th (E♭)

**FREE ACCESS** on smartphones including iPhone & Android

Using any free QR code app, scan and **HEAR** the chord

# F♯/G♭maj9

## Major 9th

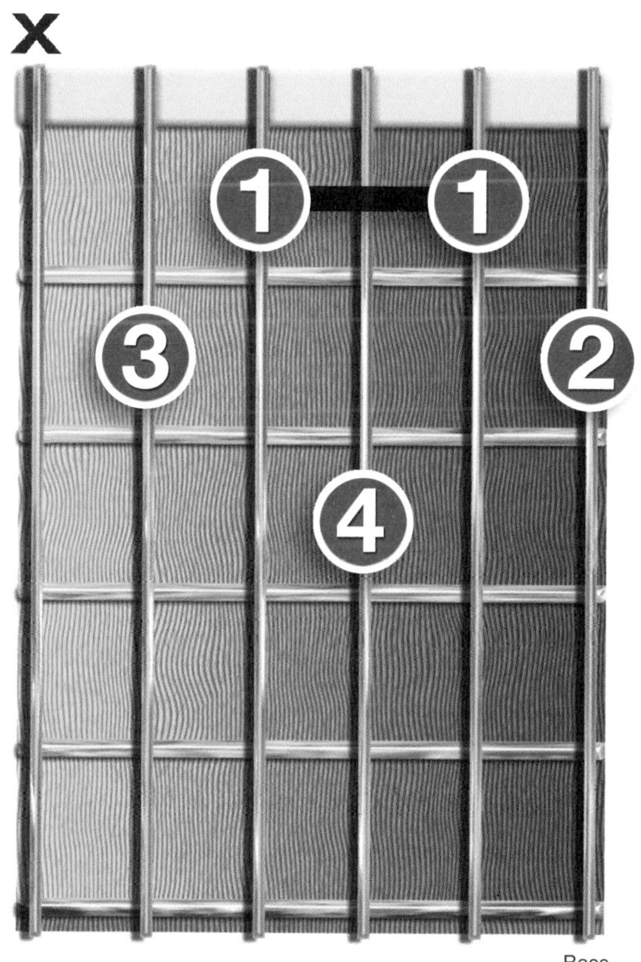


### Chord Spelling

1st (F♯), 3rd (A♯), 5th (C♯), 7th (E♯), 9th (G♯)

**FREE ACCESS** on smartphones including iPhone & Android

Using any free QR code app, scan and **HEAR** the chord

A

A♯/B♭

B

C

C♯/D♭

D

D♯/E♭

E

F

F♯/G♭

G

G♯/A♭

# G

## Major

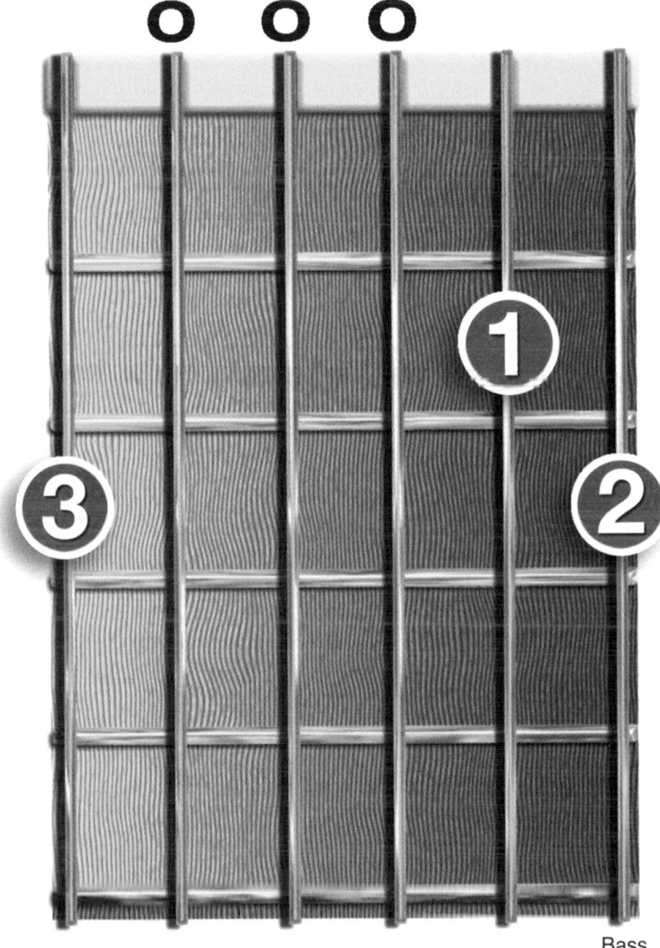


### Chord Spelling

1st (G), 3rd (B), 5th (D)

**FREE ACCESS** on smartphones including iPhone & Android

Using any free QR code app, scan and **HEAR** the chord

# Gm

## Minor

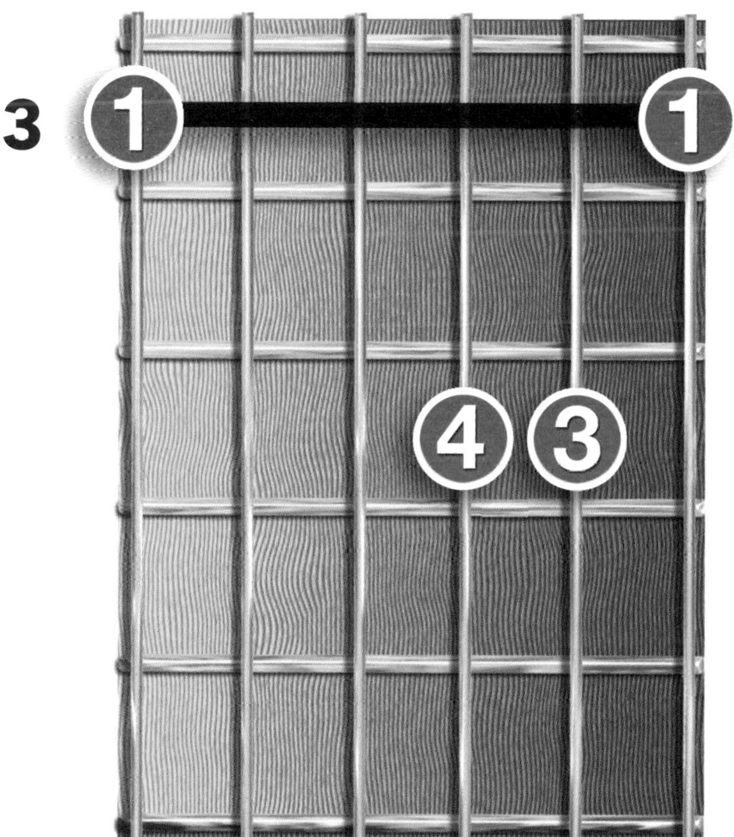


### Chord Spelling

1st (G), ♭3rd (B♭), 5th (D)

**FREE ACCESS** on smartphones including iPhone & Android

Using any free QR code app, scan and **HEAR** the chord

# G+

## Augmented Triad

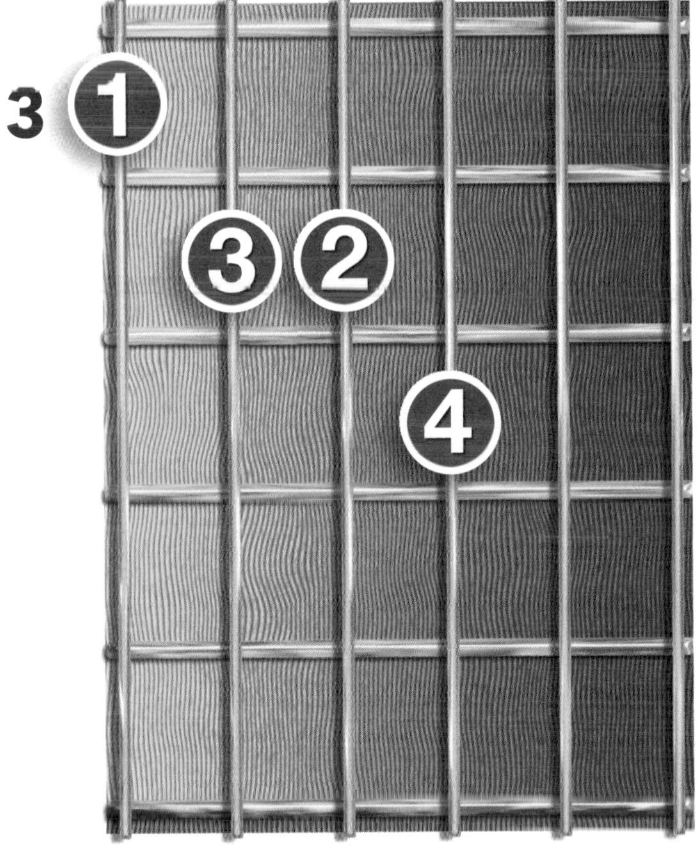


**Chord Spelling**

1st (G), 3rd (B), ♯5th (D♯)

**FREE ACCESS** on smartphones including iPhone & Android

Using any free QR code app, scan and **HEAR** the chord

# G°

## Diminished Triad

2

Bass String

### Chord Spelling

1st (G), ♭3rd (B♭), ♭5th (D♭)

G

**FREE ACCESS** on smartphones including iPhone & Android

Using any free QR code app, scan and **HEAR** the chord

# Gsus2

## Suspended 2nd

**Chord Spelling**

1st (G), 2nd (A), 5th (D)

**FREE ACCESS** on smartphones including iPhone & Android

Using any free QR code app, scan and **HEAR** the chord

# Gsus4

## Suspended 4th

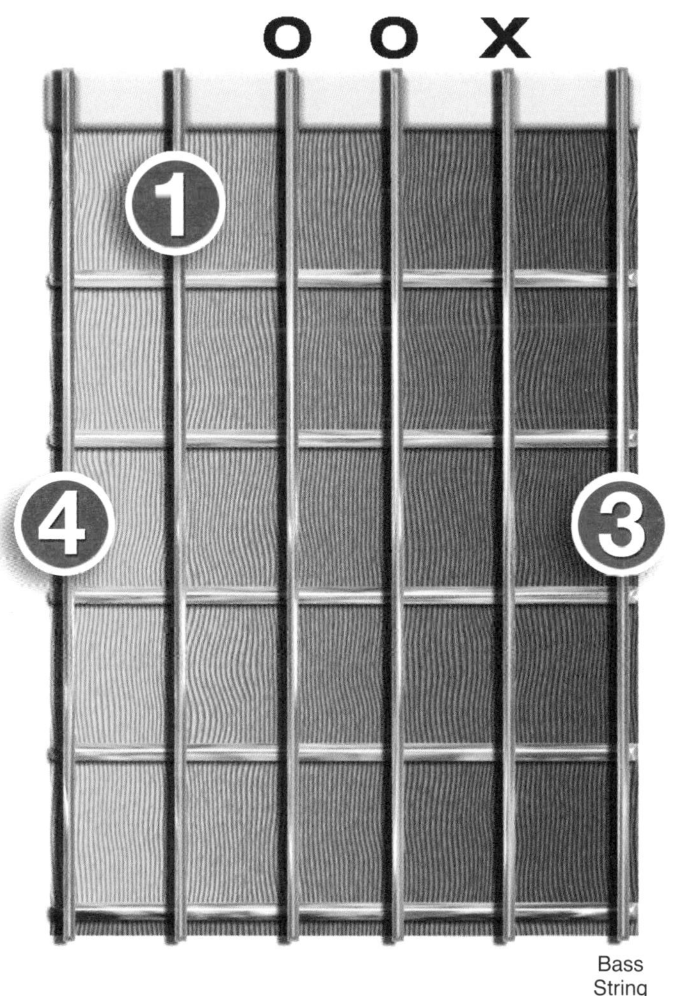


**Chord Spelling**

1st (G), 4th (C), 5th (D)

**FREE ACCESS** on smartphones including iPhone & Android

Using any free QR code app, scan and **HEAR** the chord

# G5

## 5th (Power Chord)

3

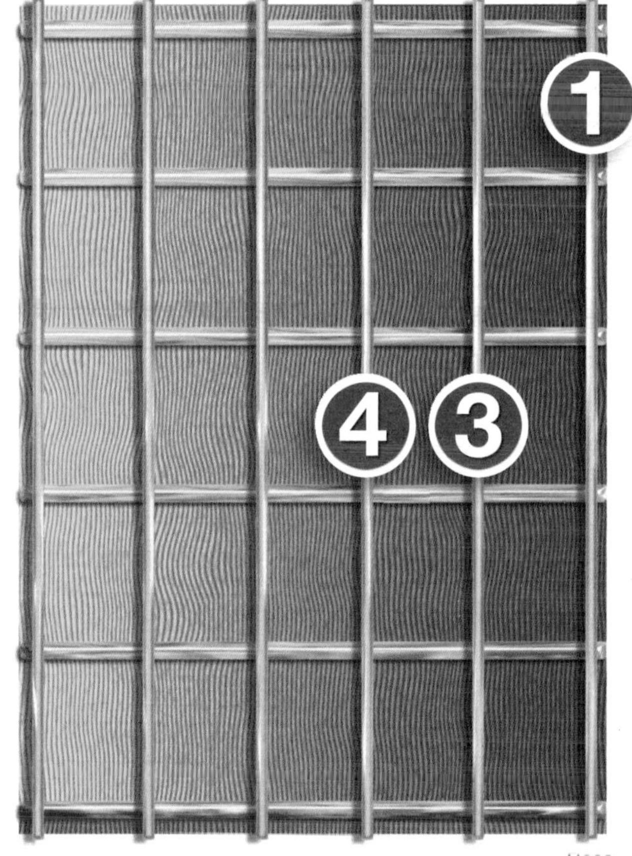


Bass
String

**Chord Spelling**

1st (G), 5th (D)

G

**FREE ACCESS** on smartphones including iPhone & Android

Using any free QR code app, scan and **HEAR** the chord

# G6

## Major 6th

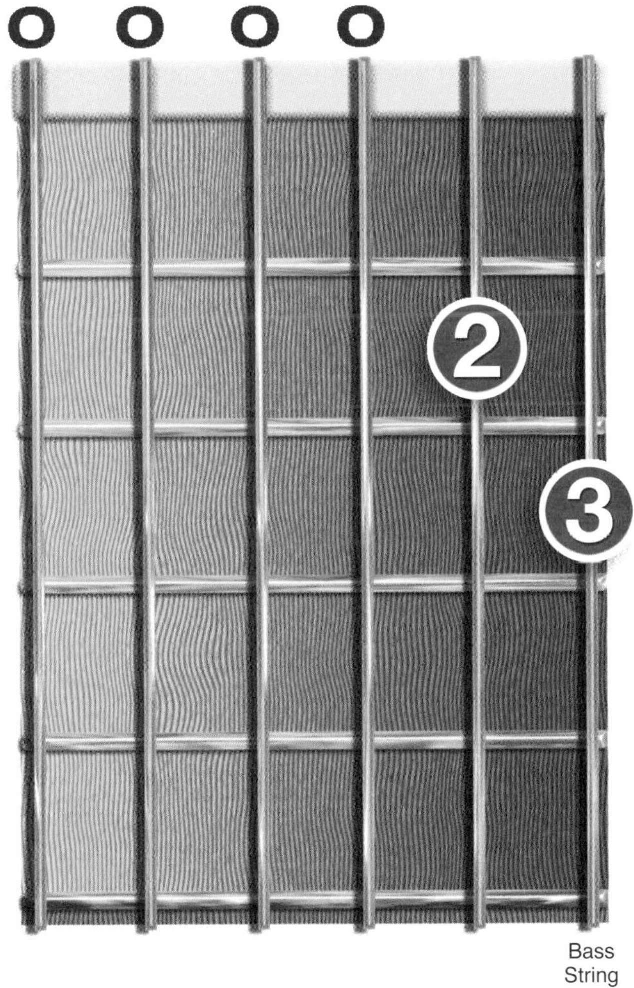


**Chord Spelling**

1st (G), 3rd (B), 5th (D), 6th (E)

G

**FREE ACCESS** on smartphones including iPhone & Android

Using any free QR code app, scan and **HEAR** the chord

# Gm6

## Minor 6th

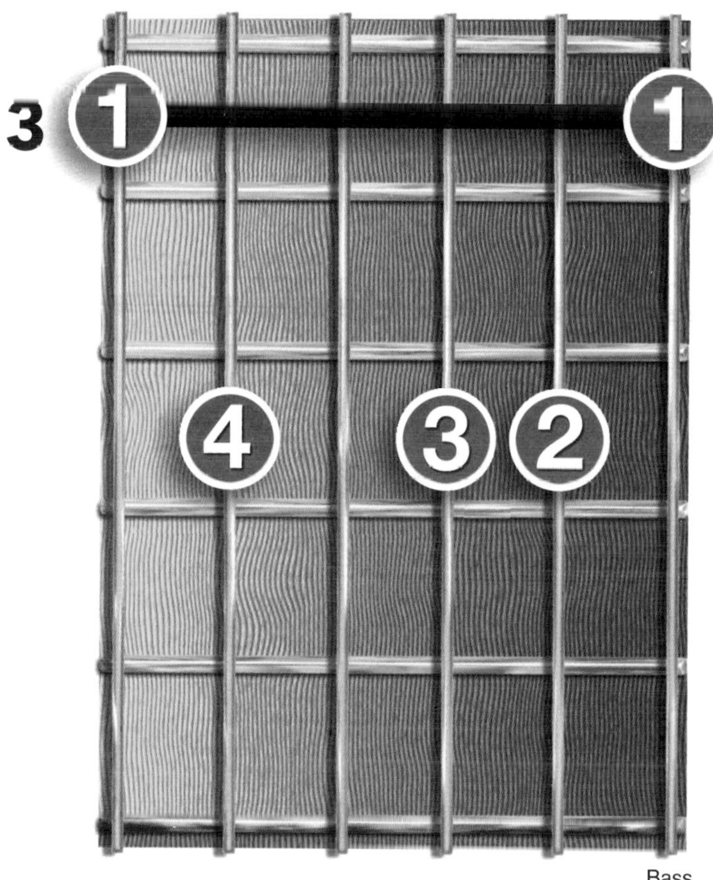


### Chord Spelling

1st (G), ♭3rd (B♭), 5th (D), 6th (E)

**FREE ACCESS** on smartphones including iPhone & Android

Using any free QR code app, scan and **HEAR** the chord

# Gmaj7

## Major 7th

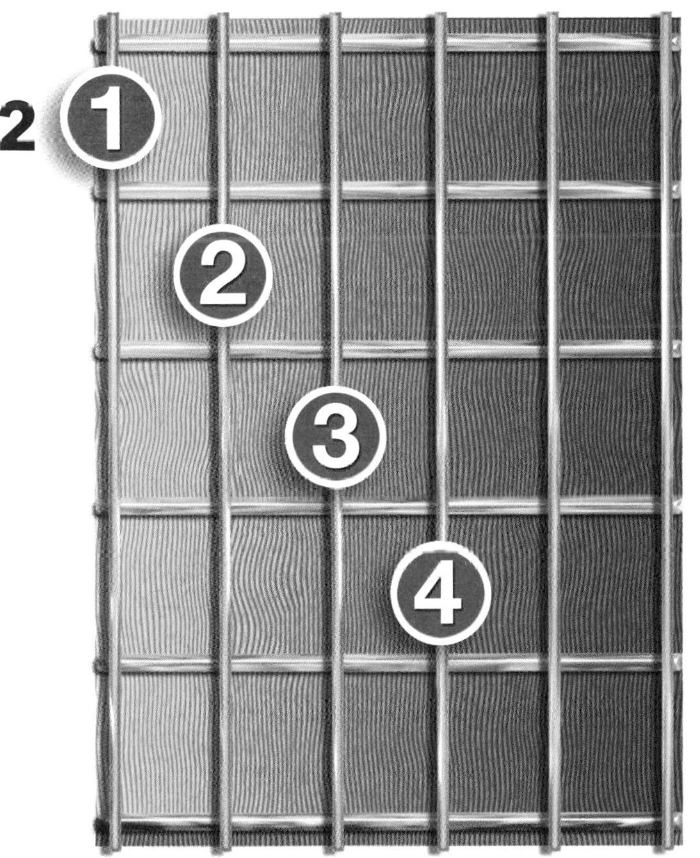


**Chord Spelling**

1st (G), 3rd (B), 5th (D), 7th (F♯)

**FREE ACCESS** on smartphones including iPhone & Android

Using any free QR code app, scan and **HEAR** the chord

G

# Gm7

## Minor 7th

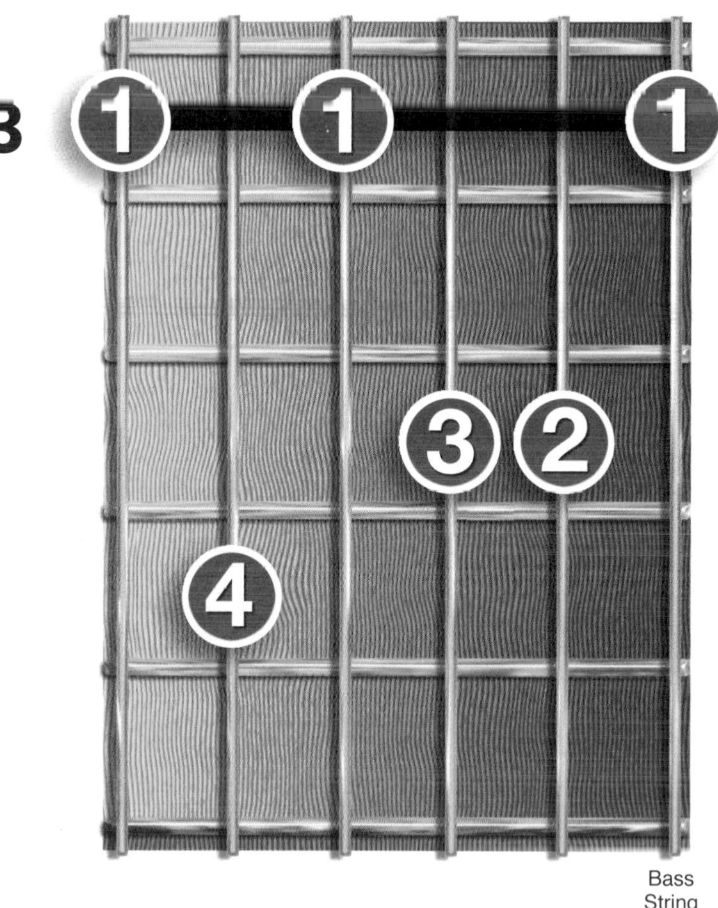


**Chord Spelling**

1st (G), ♭3rd (B♭), 5th (D), ♭7th (F)

**FREE ACCESS** on smartphones including iPhone & Android

Using any free QR code app, scan and **HEAR** the chord

# G7

## Dominant 7th

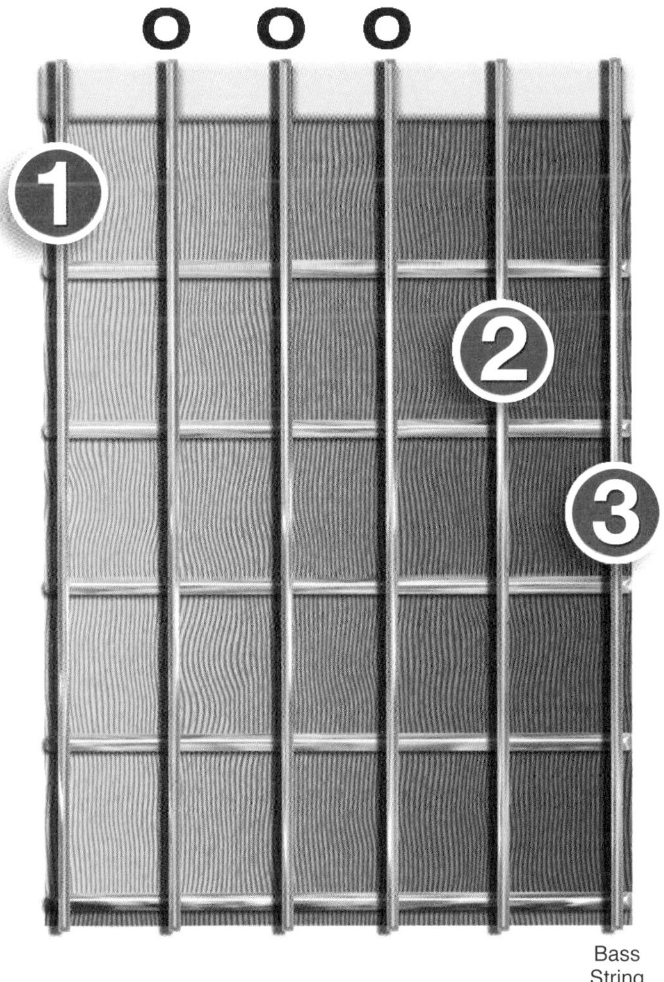


**Chord Spelling**

1st (G), 3rd (B), 5th (D), ♭7th (F)

G

**FREE ACCESS** on smartphones including iPhone & Android

Using any free QR code app, scan and **HEAR** the chord

# G°7

## Diminished 7th

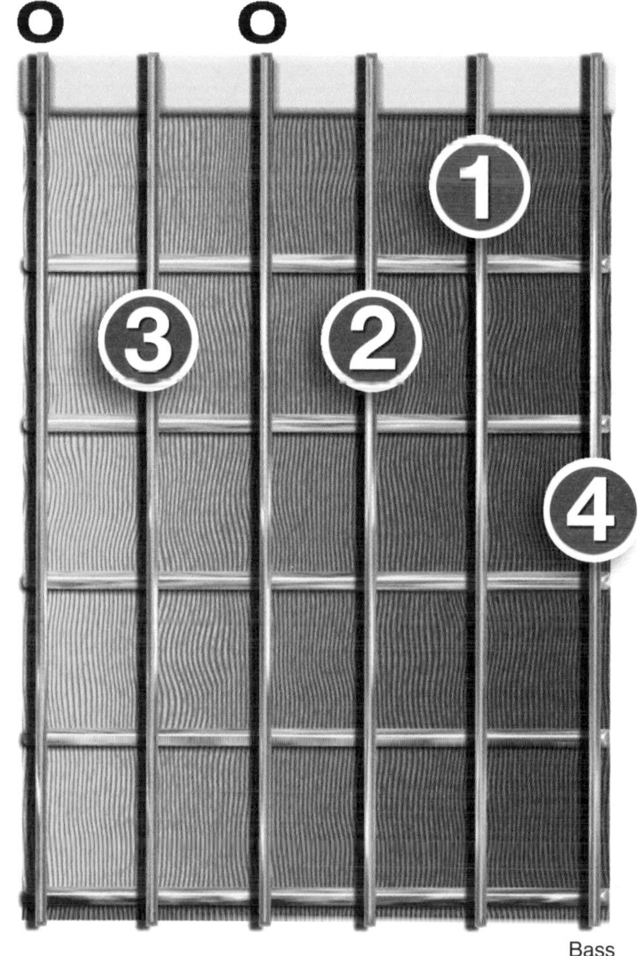


**Chord Spelling**

1st (G), ♭3rd (B♭), ♭5th (D♭), ♭♭7th (F♭)

**FREE ACCESS** on smartphones including iPhone & Android

Using any free QR code app, scan and **HEAR** the chord

# Gmaj9
## Major 9th

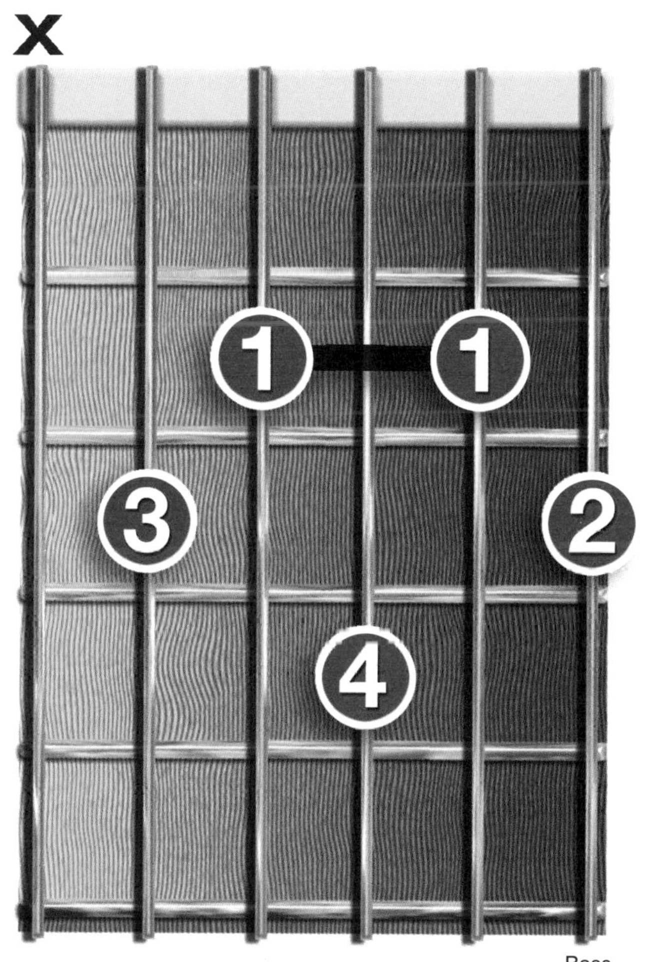


**Chord Spelling**

1st (G), 3rd (B), 5th (D), 7th (F♯), 9th (A)

**FREE ACCESS** on smartphones including iPhone & Android

Using any free QR code app, scan and **HEAR** the chord

# G♯/A♭ Major

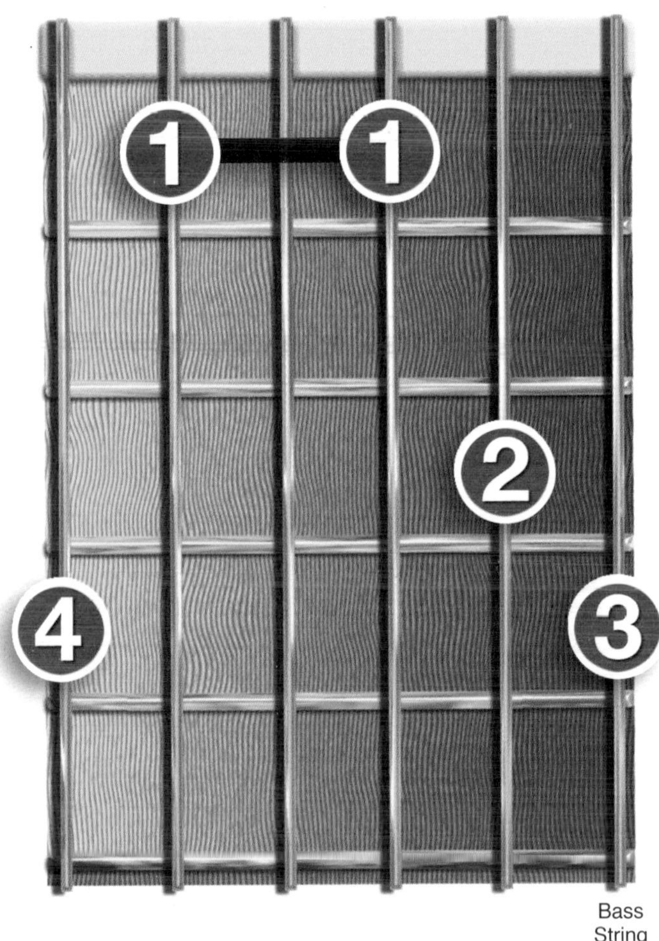


**Chord Spelling**

1st (A♭), 3rd (C), 5th (E♭)

**FREE ACCESS** on smartphones including iPhone & Android

Using any free QR code app, scan and **HEAR** the chord

# G♯/A♭m
## Minor

**Chord Spelling**

1st (A♭), ♭3rd (C♭), 5th (E♭)

**FREE ACCESS** on smartphones including iPhone & Android

Using any free QR code app, scan and **HEAR** the chord

# G♯/A♭+

## Augmented Triad

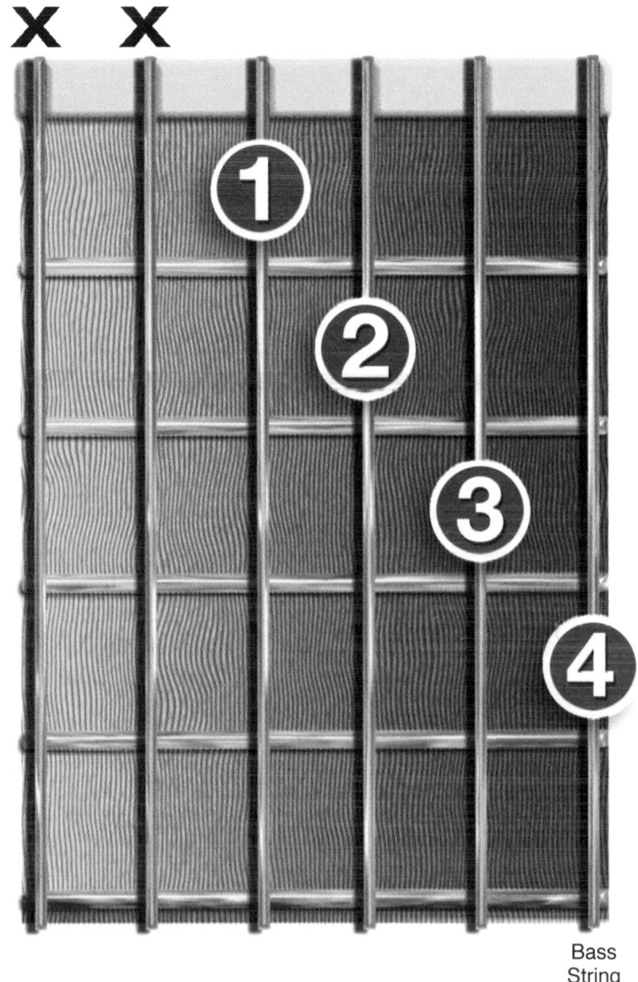


### Chord Spelling

1st (A♭), 3rd (C), ♯5th (E)

**FREE ACCESS** on smartphones including iPhone & Android

Using any free QR code app, scan and **HEAR** the chord

# G♯/A♭°

## Diminished Triad

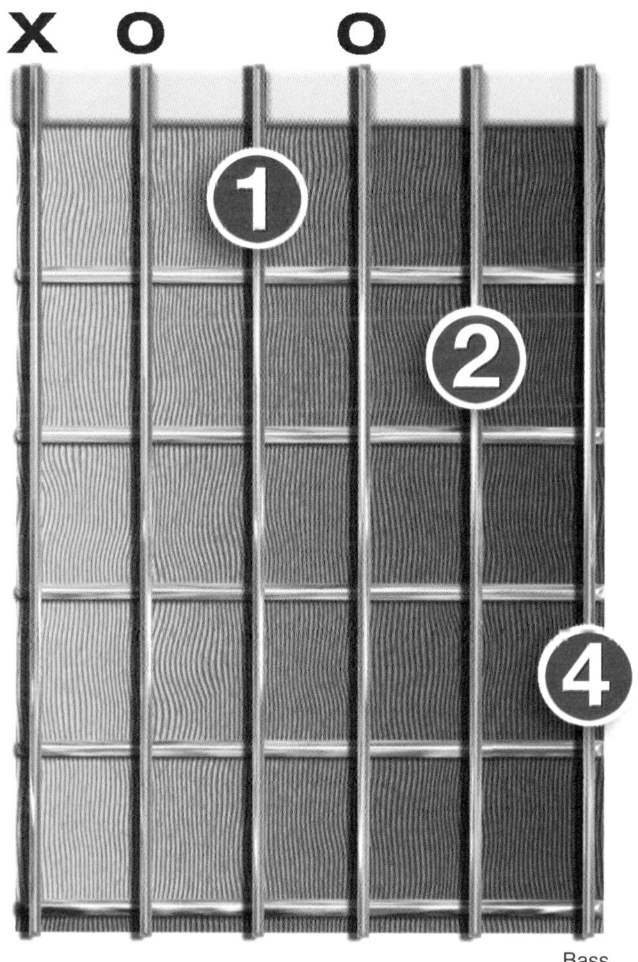


**Chord Spelling**

1st (A♭), ♭3rd (C♭), ♭5th (E♭♭)

**FREE ACCESS** on smartphones including iPhone & Android

Using any free QR code app, scan and **HEAR** the chord

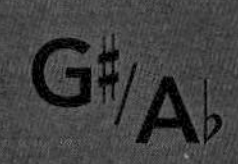

# G♯/A♭sus2
## Suspended 2nd

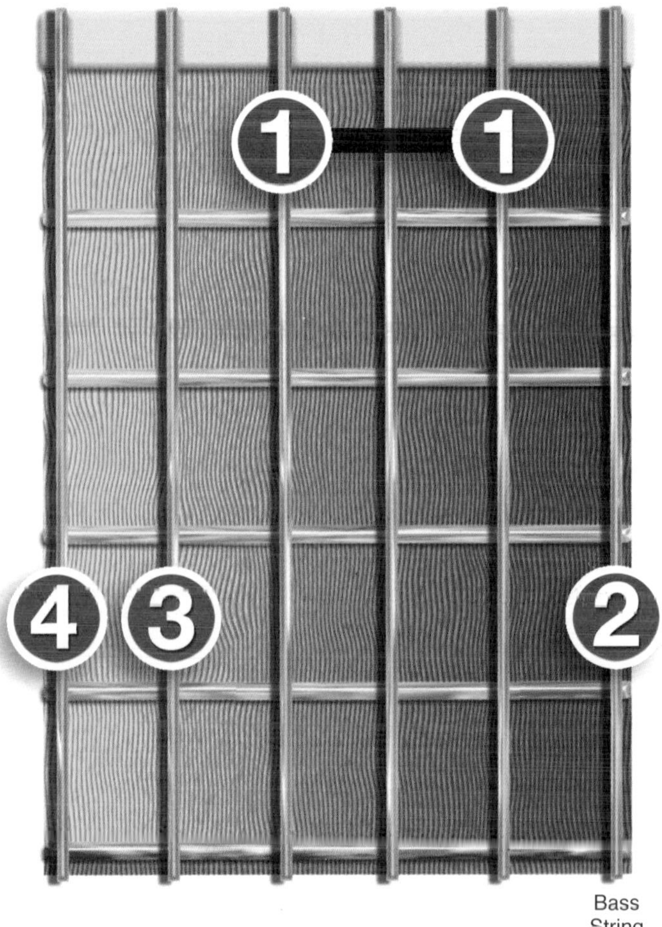


**Chord Spelling**

1st (A♭), 2nd (B♭), 5th (E♭)

**FREE ACCESS** on smartphones including iPhone & Android

Using any free QR code app, scan and **HEAR** the chord

# G♯/A♭sus4

## Suspended 4th

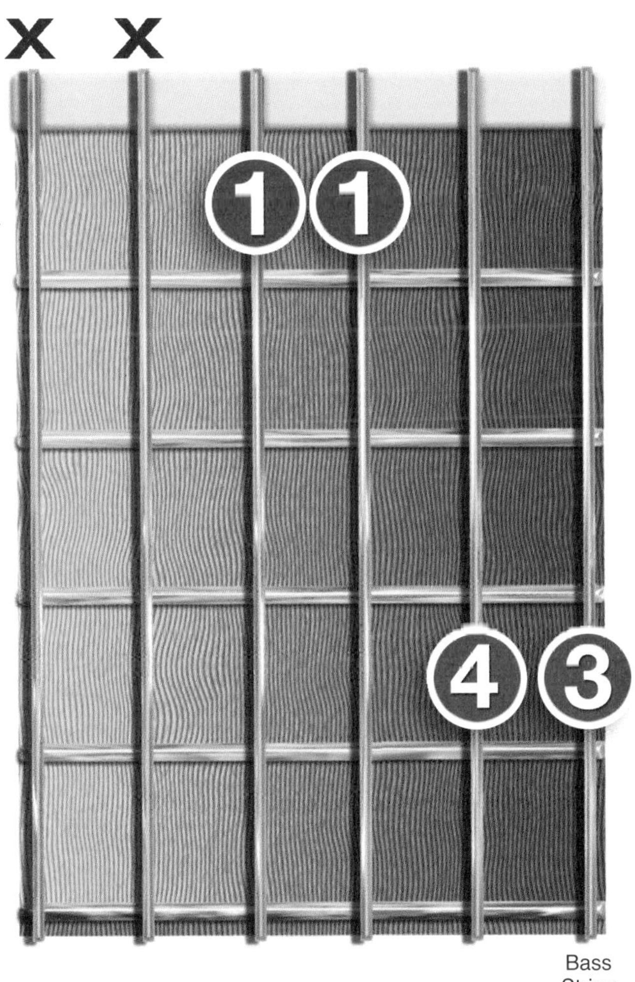


### Chord Spelling

1st (A♭), 4th (D♭), 5th (E♭)

**FREE ACCESS** on smartphones including iPhone & Android

Using any free QR code app, scan and **HEAR** the chord

# G♯/A♭5

## 5th (Power Chord)

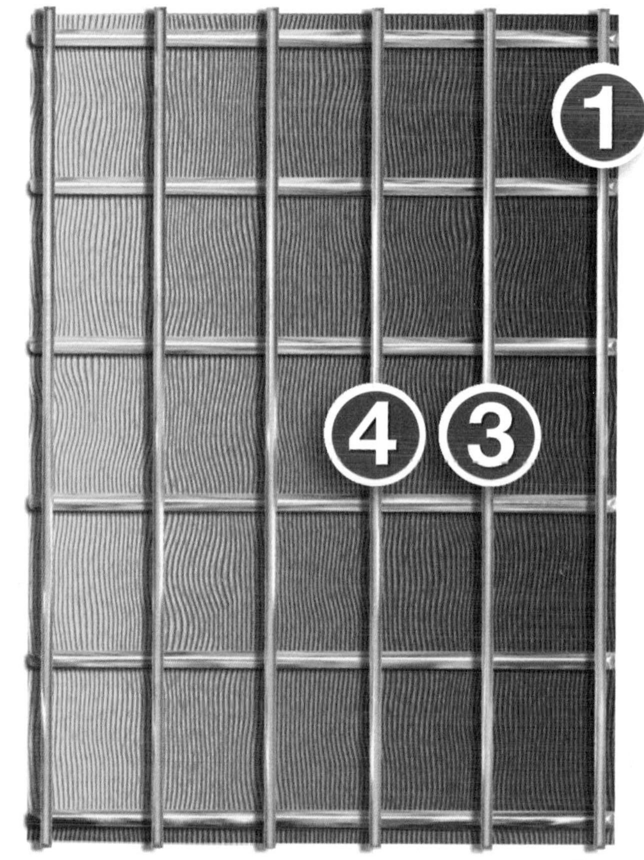


### Chord Spelling

1st (A♭), 5th (E♭)

**FREE ACCESS** on smartphones including iPhone & Android

Using any free QR code app, scan and **HEAR** the chord

# G♯/A♭6
## Major 6th

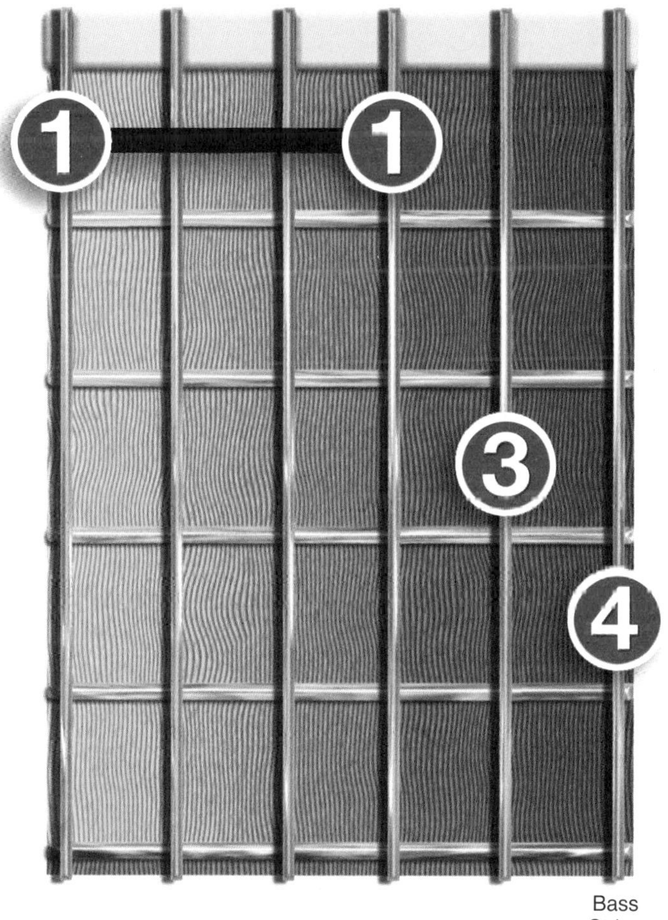


### Chord Spelling

1st (A♭), 3rd (C), 5th (E♭), 6th (F)

**FREE ACCESS** on smartphones including iPhone & Android

Using any free QR code app, scan and **HEAR** the chord

# G♯/A♭m6
## Minor 6th

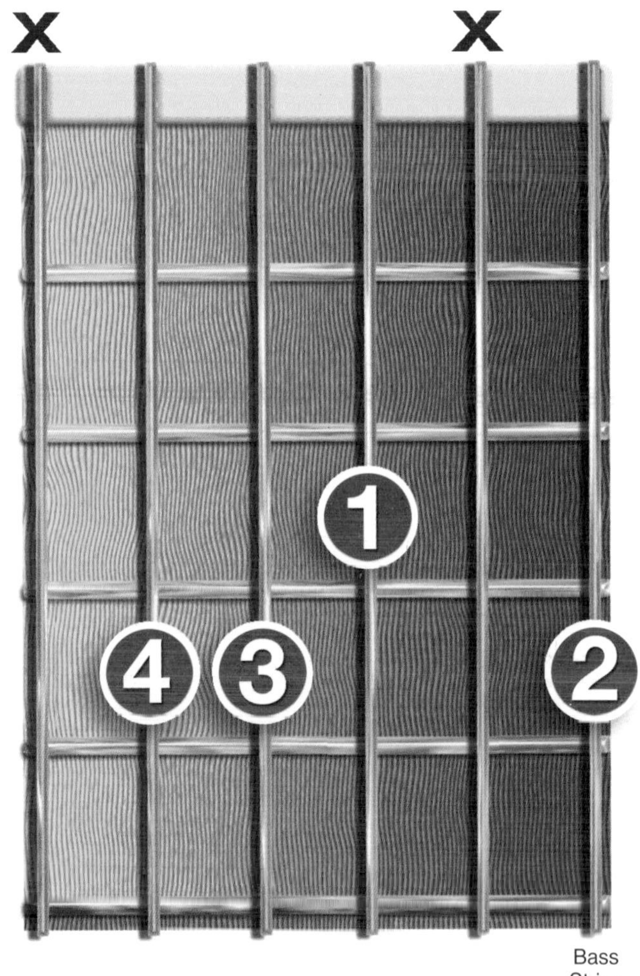


**Chord Spelling**

1st (A♭), ♭3rd (C♭), 5th (E♭), 6th (F)

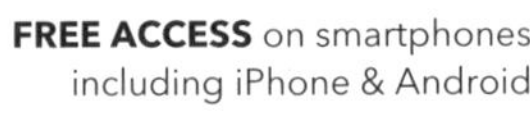
**FREE ACCESS** on smartphones including iPhone & Android

Using any free QR code app, scan and **HEAR** the chord

# G♯/A♭maj7

## Major 7th

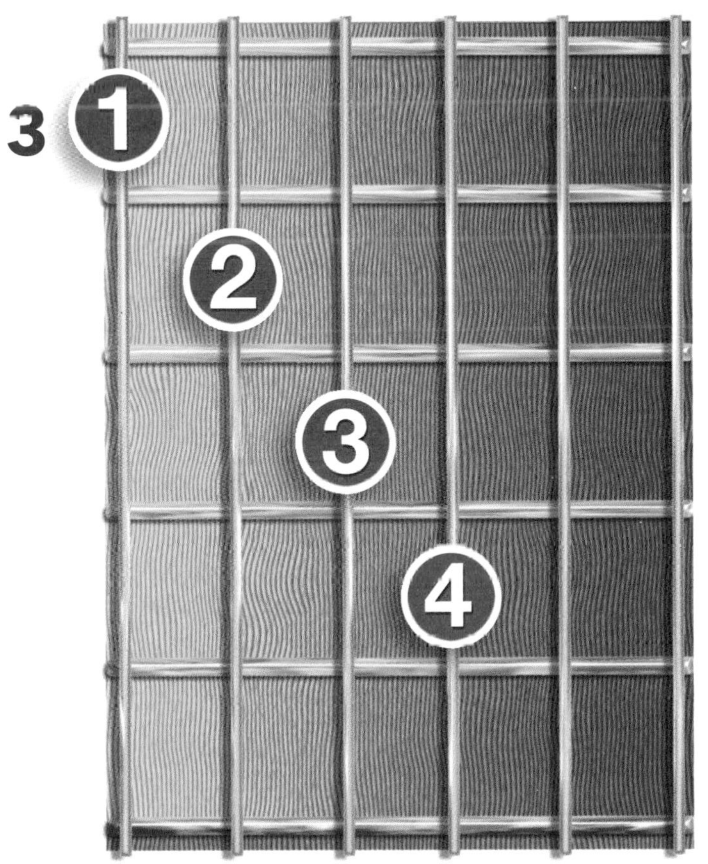


Bass String

**Chord Spelling**

1st (A♭), 3rd (C), 5th (E♭), 7th (G)

**FREE ACCESS** on smartphones including iPhone & Android

Using any free QR code app, scan and **HEAR** the chord

A
A♯/B♭
B
C
C♯/D♭
D
D♯/E♭
E
F
F♯/G♭
G
G♯/A♭

# G♯/A♭m7

## Minor 7th

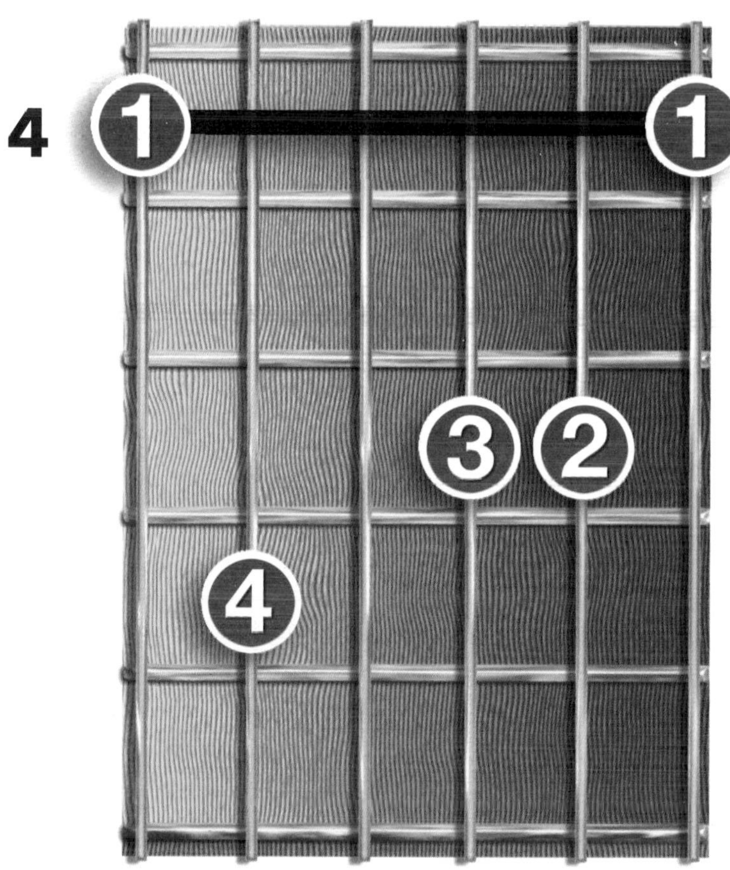


Bass String

**Chord Spelling**

1st (A♭), ♭3rd (C♭), 5th (E♭), ♭7th (G♭)

**FREE ACCESS** on smartphones including iPhone & Android

Using any free QR code app, scan and **HEAR** the chord

# G♯/A♭7

## Dominant 7th

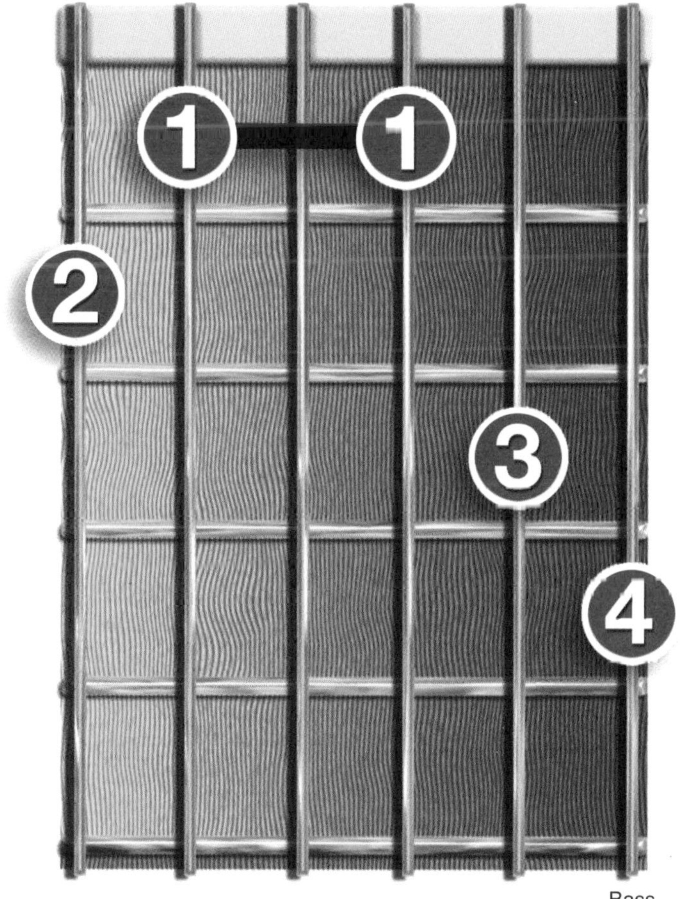


### Chord Spelling

1st (A♭), 3rd (C), 5th (E♭), ♭7th (G♭)

**FREE ACCESS** on smartphones including iPhone & Android

Using any free QR code app, scan and **HEAR** the chord

# G♯/A♭°7

## Diminished 7th

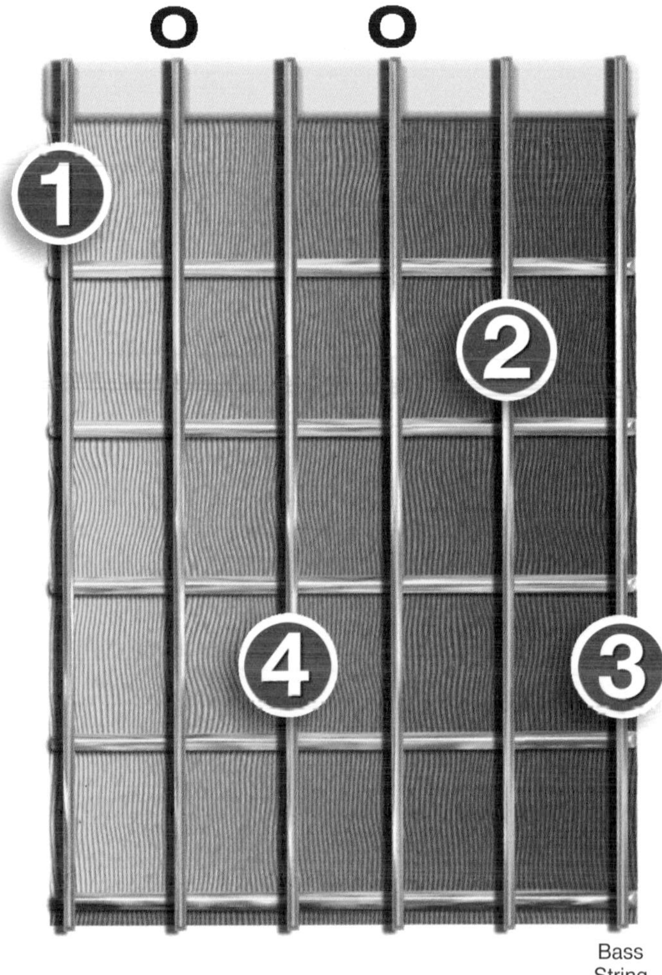


**Chord Spelling**

1st (A♭), ♭3rd (C♭), ♭5th (E♭♭), ♭♭7th (G♭♭)

**FREE ACCESS** on smartphones including iPhone & Android

Using any free QR code app, scan and **HEAR** the chord

# G♯/A♭maj9
## Major 9th

3

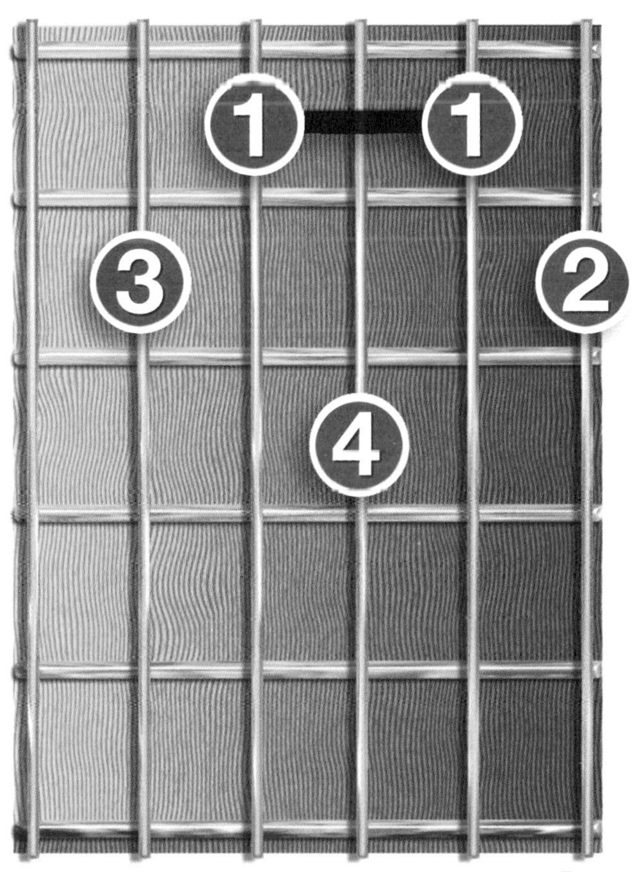


Bass
String

**Chord Spelling**

1st (A♭), 3rd (C), 5th (E♭), 7th (G), 9th (B♭)

**FREE ACCESS** on smartphones including iPhone & Android

Using any free QR code app, scan and **HEAR** the chord

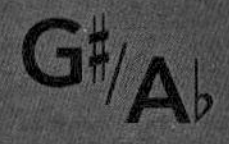

# flametreemusic.com

**The Flame Tree Music website complements our range of print books and offers easy access to chords and scales online, and on the move, through tablets, smartphones, and desktop computers.**

1. The site offers access to chord diagrams and finger positions for both the guitar and the piano/keyboard, presenting a wide range of sound options to help develop good listening technique, and to assist you in identifying the chord and each note within it.

2. The site offers 12 **free** chords, those most commonly used in bands and songwriting.

3. A subscription is available if you'd like the full range of chords, **50** for **each key**.

4. Guitar chords are shown with **first** and **second positions on the fretboard**.

5. For the keyboard, you can **see** and **hear** each note in **left**- and **right-hand positions**.

6. Choose the key, then the chord name from the drop down menu. Note that the **red chords** are available **free**. Those in blue can be accessed with a subscription.

7. Once you've selected the chord, press **GO** and the details of the chord will be shown, with chord spellings, keyboard and guitar fingerings.

8. Sounds are provided in four easy-to-understand configurations.

9. flametreemusic.com also gives you access to **20 scales for each key**.

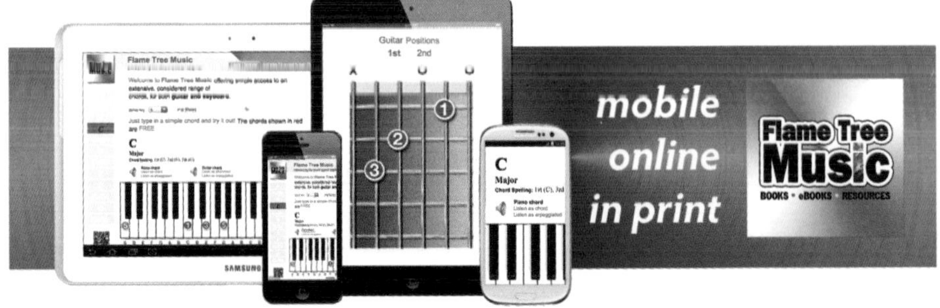